TIME
IS
RUNNING
SHORT

Sid Roth

Destiny Image Publishers
P.O. Box 351
Shippensburg, PA 17257
"Speaking to the Purposes of God for this Generation"

ISBN 1-56043-030-3

For Worldwide Distribution
Printed in the U.S.A.

Messianic Vision
P.O. Box 34444
Bethesda, MD 20827

First Printing: 1990
Second Printing: 1991

NEW ADDRESS:
MESSIANIC VISION
P.O. Box 1918
BRUNSWICK, GEORGIA 31521-1918
(912) 265-2500

DEDICATION

To my mother, who demonstrated God's love by her life. Shalom, Le'hitra'ot (goodbye and I'll see you again), Mom.

ACKNOWLEDGEMENTS

This book would not have been possible without the input of many men and women of God in my life. I want to thank Manny Brotman who taught me Messianic Jewish evangelism; Ari and Shira Sorko-Ram, whose lives as Israeli pioneers and whose teaching have greatly influenced me; Robert DuVall for editing the manuscript; and my gift from God — my wife, Joy.

CONTENTS

FOREWORD

By Dr. Derek Prince

(Questions by Sid Roth)

Sid Roth:

How does someone like yourself, a university professor born in England, from a non-Jewish background, have such a Jewish burden?

Dr. Prince:

Well it ties in with my life story. I was a professor at Cambridge in philosophy; I was not interested in religion. Since I'd been compelled to go to church in my school-going years and I'd concluded that Christianity didn't have the answer, I was looking elsewhere for answers. That's why I became a philosopher. But when I was drafted into the British army in 1940, I had one big problem — what am I going to take with me to read? because reading was really my life. So I bought myself a nice new black Bible and took it with me into the army. Well, I found it to be a very baffling, wearisome book. I couldn't get any real inspiration or illumination from it. But I said to myself, "No book is going to beat me. I've started; I'm going to read it."

About nine months later when I was somewhere in the middle of the book of Job, which is pretty good progress for a nonbeliever, I had a personal encounter with somebody in the middle of the night. I was in an army barrack room where no one else was awake, and I found myself calling out to this unknown person who I knew was there. "Unless you bless me, I will not let you go." God moved in and met me, and I had an overwhelming experience of supernatural power that lasted more than one hour. Without any active participation of my will, I was a totally changed person from that night on. That was 49 years ago, so you could say the change has been permanent.

Sid Roth:

How did you move then into having such a Jewish heart?

Dr. Prince:

Well, there again it was through circumstances. very soon after that experience, my unit was sent overseas to the Middle East. I spent the next four and a half years in the Middle East — two years in Egypt and Libya, one year in the Sudan and then a year and a half in the country that was then called Palestine. I got to Palestine just about the time the news of the holocaust was filtering through to the Jewish people in Palestine. By that time in my study of the Bible, I'd gotten to the prophets — Isaiah, Jeremiah, Ezekiel — and I was pretty familiar with what they were saying. When I arrived in Palestine and began to associate with Jewish people, I said to myself, "This is like reading the day's newspaper. What those prophets wrote is happening right in front of my eyes." So I began to see the reality of the Bible's prophecies concerning the restoration of Israel.

After I was released from the army, I married a Danish lady who had a small childrens' home; I continued in Palestine as head of that home. Also, when I was married, I automatically became a father to a family of eight girls — six Jewish, one Arab and one English. We were living in Jewish Jerusalem just a short distance from the old city when the first Arab-Israeli war broke out, the War of Independence. Again I witnessed miracles because I knew how feeble were the resources of the Jewish people and how immensely outnumbered they were by the Arabs. Basically, there were about 650,000 Jews opposed by about 40 million Arabs — six Arab states with modern armies and equipment. The Jewish soldiers, on the other hand, had very scratchy equipment that they'd scrounged or stolen or imported.

All the experts believed they wouldn't survive. But there's never been any area about which experts have so often been wrong as the Middle East. The fact is they did survive. And I was an eyewitness of that miracle of history.

I remember Jewish soldiers saying: "We just can't understand it. We go into a place where there are Arabs who outnumber us and are better armed, but it's just as if they're paralyzed." Although that was an amazing statement, I think it was really the most accurate way to sum up what took place. There was a supernatural power at work that assisted the Jews.

As you know, Israel emerged from that war a sovereign state. Again I said to myself, "This is what I've been reading in the prophets — Isaiah 66:8: 'a nation born in a day.' " It all happened in front of my eyes. I had no previous conception of it, no theories about it, no understanding of prophecy. But the events made it so real and vivid to me that from then on I've always believed that the record of the prophets, which is, incidentally, confirmed in the New Testament, is the reliable guide concerning what's going on in our world today.

Sid Roth:

Derek, there are many people who might say about you, "I understand how Derek Prince could have a warm spot in his heart for the Jewish people and Israel because of the circumstances that you have described. Under the new covenant, however, we're new creations. God's not any more interested in Jerusalem, Israel, than He is in Paris, France. He's interested in all places." What would you say to someone like that?

Dr. Prince:

Well, I'm interested in all places too. As you know, I have a worldwide radio Bible teaching program as well as a ministry that distributes Bible teaching material. We are now reaching 126 nations. And interestingly enough, while I was in the Sudan, the first person I ever led to the Lord was a Moslem. So I've never been narrow-minded or exclusive in my view. On the other hand, I do think that the Jewish people and the land of Israel and the city of Jerusalem occupy a unique place in God's plan. Otherwise the Bible is a misleading book.

Furthermore, I believe that good evidence of the genuine conversion of a Gentile is that he loves the Jews. Likewise, good evidence of the conversion of a Jew is that he loves Gentiles.

Sid Roth:

I like that, but I want to pin you down for a second. What if a Gentile that is genuinely born again doesn't have any particular love for the Jews and Israel?

Dr. Prince:

Well he's deficient. I mean, he's incomplete.

INTRODUCTION

More than sixteen million Soviet Jews[1] *are slated for execution.* I have just returned from a fact-finding trip to the Soviet Union. The situation is worse than I expected. Not only are there huge shortages, but everything the Soviets have built is literally falling apart. With all these problems a scapegoat is needed. Who has been chosen? From Soviet intellectuals to skinheads there is a consensus — the enemy is the Jew.

Have you ever wondered, "Why do so many people hate the Jews?" Before Jesus came, the answer to this question was simple: Satan was using any means at his disposal to annihilate the people who would give birth to the Messiah. But why is satan *still trying* to destroy the Jews? And why should this concern Christians? BECAUSE THE JEWISH PEOPLE HOLD THE KEY TO EVANGELIZING THE WORLD, TO MESSIAH'S RETURN AND TO SATAN'S FINAL DEFEAT.

In Matthew 23:39, Jesus tells us the LAST BIBLICAL EVENT necessary before His return: "For I tell you, you will not see Me again until you say, 'Blessed is He who comes in the name of the Lord.'" Jesus will not return — and satan will not be put out of the way — until the Jewish people recognize Jesus as Messiah.

1. Soviet Jewish authorities estimate there are over sixteen million Soviet Jews with at least 25% Jewish blood.

Just as Jews were used mightily to initiate the gospel at the first coming of Jesus, they will be raised up as mighty witnesses to evangelize the world just before His return. Isaiah 2:3 tells us that in the last days " . . . the word of the LORD [will go out] from Jerusalem." Fiery end-time Jewish evangelists are now being prepared who will once again turn the world upside down with the good news of the Messiah.

The Jew not only is essential to Messiah's return but also is God's instrument to bless — and curse — individuals and nations. God tells Abraham in Genesis 12:3:

I will bless those who bless you, and whoever curses you I will curse; and all peoples on earth will be blessed through you.

Jesus also says that all nations will be judged according to their actions toward the Jews.

When the Son of Man comes in his glory, and all the angels with him, he will sit on his throne in heavenly glory. All the nations will be gathered before him, and HE WILL SEPARATE THE PEOPLE ONE FROM ANOTHER AS A SHEPHERD SEPARATES THE SHEEP FROM THE GOATS (Matt. 25:31,32).

Do you know the major difference between a sheep and a goat? A goat has a mind of its own, while a sheep follows the shepherd. What will be the *single issue* of obedience that will cause this distinction? The issue of division is found in Matthew 25:40. Jesus, our Shepherd, says: "Whatever you did for one of the least of these brothers of mine, you did for me." Who are His brothers? In context, He is speaking of His brothers after the flesh, the Jewish people. Yes, you can apply this promise to the future spiritual seed of Abraham (Christians), but at that moment in time He was clearly talking about the physical Jew. Even the Greek word used here for "brother" literally means, "from the womb."

The whole world is out of kilter when the Jew is out of God's predetermined plan. Even the boundaries of nations are based on the Jewish nation being in place.

When the Most High gave the nations their inheritance, when he divided all mankind, he set up boundaries for the peoples according to the number of the sons of Israel (Deut. 32:8).

When the Jews are out of God's assigned boundaries (Israel) they are under a curse (Deut. 28:36). Conversely, God says He will bless the Jewish people when they are in the land (Deut. 28:8b). But not only the Jewish people will be blessed when they are in place physically and spiritually; the whole world will be blessed. In that day, Israel will become like the garden of Eden (Ezek.36:35)! And the Messiah will rule the world from Jerusalem (Zech. 14).

NO WONDER SATAN AND HIS FOLLOWERS ARE TRYING TO ELIMINATE THE JEWS!

But just as satan has a strategy to destroy all the Jewish people, God has a strategy to preserve them. Perhaps the best presentation of the conflict between these two strategies and its inevitable conclusion is contained in the book of Esther where God delivered His people from an enemy bent on their total destruction.

As recently as this century, the theme of Esther was recreated with amazing accuracy. In March 1953, Joseph Stalin developed a master plan to murder all the Soviet Jews.[2] But like Haman in

2. H.L. Wilmington, *Wilmington's Guide to the Bible* (Wheaton, IL: Tyndale House Publishing, 1988), p. 253.

the book of Esther, Stalin died before the plan could be implemented. Ironically, he was buried on Purim, the day Jews celebrate their great victory over Haman. However, *the same spirit found in Haman and Stalin is still manipulating world events to try to destroy the Jew.*

Today, God is calling His Church to stand up for the Jewish people. In this and many other respects, Esther is a type of the end-time Church. Just as Esther was adopted by a Jewish family, Gentile believers have been grafted into the family of Abraham through the Jewish Messiah. And, like Esther, Gentile believers have a strategic role to play in the preservation of the Jewish people and the return of Jesus. No less than the salvation of the world is contingent on the salvation of Israel!

This book is divided into four parts. The first part shows the parallels between Esther and today's Church and explains the destiny of the Church in bringing about the salvation of Israel. The second part allows you to eavesdrop as I share the Messiah with my Jewish parents. This will give you a heart sensitivity and understanding of my people. The third part will teach you to share Yeshua (Jesus) with God's chosen people. And the final part answers the question, "Is the Church the 'New Israel'?" After you complete this book, you will know more about the Messiah than 99% of the Jewish people, including rabbis!

My hope and prayer is that this book will equip and encourage you to assume your God-given "Esther" role by reaching out to Jewish people with the love of Messiah and by joining the battle against satan's efforts to annihilate God's chosen people. "And who knows but that you have come to royal position for such a time as this?" (Esth. 4:14b).

PART I

FOR SUCH

A TIME AS THIS

CHAPTER ONE:

ESTHER — A TYPE OF THE END-TIME CHURCH

ESTHER (CHURCH), LIKE ESTHER OF OLD, YOU HAVE A DESTINY TO FULFILL. YOU WERE CREATED TO DO BATTLE ON BEHALF OF THE JEWISH PEOPLE. BE PREPARED FOR YOUR GREATEST HOUR.

God's Master Strategy

God's master end-time strategy is revealed in the book of Esther. Allegorically speaking, Esther represents the end-time Church. Esther was adopted into a Jewish family. She was an orphan without father or mother. Esther was a flawless, beautiful, young virgin. She had favor with the king. And Esther was totally obedient. She was also instructed to keep her Jewish identity hidden.

3

Do you know another Esther who is also a flawless, beautiful, young, virgin? When God looks at one of His born-from-above children, He sees no flaws, blemishes or sin. As God's child you are as righteous as Jesus. Esther (Church), you are beautiful in His sight. You are God's workmanship, created in His image. You are as loved, appreciated and accepted as Jesus.

At the beginning of the book of Esther, we read that the queen of the land was rebellious. In fact, that is what her name, Vashti, means. In this kingdom, the queen had to be subject to the complete will of the king. Because Vashti was not willing to submit, she was removed and a search was conducted for a new queen.

What was the chance of Esther, an orphan without the proper heritage, becoming queen of the land? That was how much chance the Gentiles had of being grafted spiritually into the seed of Abraham. Yet, neither happened by "chance," but by God's divine plan.

Crushing Yields the Spectacular

Esther had to be prepared for her new responsibility. Part of her preparation was to bathe for six months in oil of myrrh. The myrrh plant is not sweet on the outside, but when it is *crushed* the fragrance is spectacular.

Paul learned that through faith and patience either the problem would change or God would change him. And change he did! Listen to a man who has been molded into Messiah's image:

I have been crucified with [Messiah] and I no longer live, but [Messiah] lives in me. The life I live in the body, I live by faith in

4

the Son of God, who loved me and gave himself for me (Gal. 2:20).

The fragrance coming from Paul was pure Jesus. And, like Esther, he was completely obedient. In the midst of adversity he would be filled with joy. People were watching him. Would he complain and murmur when circumstances were bad? Or would he react based on the pure truth of the Word? As people watched his childlike faith, they were provoked to jealousy. What he had, they wanted. Church, it is time to walk in supernatural joy all the time. It is time to worry for nothing. It is time to start provoking the Jewish people and all people to jealousy.

Don't Give Up!

Esther did not become queen right away. It took four years before she was even considered by the king. I am glad she did not give up. Church, don't give up! The King is molding you into His image. Not only are people watching you, but angels, demons, those who have died, the devil and God are watching you. It is as though you are an actor on a stage and the whole world wants to see if you will be faithful to God no matter what the circumstances.

God has promised never to leave you or forsake you. He has promised to forgive you. He has promised to keep you in perfect peace in this life. He has promised that His grace is sufficient for all circumstances. He has promised to provide for every one of your needs. He has provided healing for all your diseases. He has given you the authority to use the name of Jesus. He has given you His wisdom. And He has promised to personally escort you to heaven. So, Esther, hold up your head and walk like the child of royalty you are.

Esther Could Keep a Secret

God gave Esther favor and approval with the king, and she was grafted into royalty. Although she was now the queen, she still honored Mordecai, the one who had raised her, by keeping secret her family and Jewish background. Esther might have argued with Mordecai and said, "Now that I am the queen, I want to tell the king about my family." I am glad she was obedient because, had she opened her mouth, Mordecai would not have overheard two royal guards conspiring to kill the king. The guards ignored Mordecai because they were unaware of his relationship to Esther. Later, Mordecai alerted Esther, who in turn reported the conspiracy to the king.

Esther could have taken responsibility for the heroics, but instead gave full credit to Mordecai.[3] Do you know what reward Mordecai got for saving the king's life? His name was written in the records of the king. He received no money or recognition, not even an article in the Susa Times! Mordecai could have turned bitter. Instead, he looked to God for his reward. Later on, God used this incident to save Mordecai's life.

3. "Do not withhold good from those who deserve it, when it is in your power to act" (Prov. 3:27).

6

Silver for Jews

Haman's name means "rager," "mad one" and "angry." This describes what happened when Mordecai refused to kneel down before him. Haman became so enraged he looked for a way to kill not just Mordecai, but *all* Jews.

Haman tried to convince those in authority that it was not in their best interest to tolerate the Jew. And to make his proposal more attractive, he offered the king millions of dollars worth of silver. It reminds me of the Arab oil embargo a few years ago. Do you remember the long lines for gas? Signs began to surface that read, "Dump Israel; we want gas!"

The Key to Esther's Success

Esther (the Church) will not counter satan's moves by just taking up offerings, as was Esther's first plan when she heard Mordecai was fasting, weeping and in sackcloth. Clothing was the last thing Mordecai needed. Finally, Esther got the message. Fasting, humility and prayer were the only things that would save the lives of the Jews.

When the prayer and fasting started, satan knew he was in trouble. He had to work fast.

First, he had to kill Esther. When Mordecai commanded her to go to the king, satan thought he had her. It was the law of the land that no queen could go to the king unless he requested her presence. The king had not requested her presence for thirty days. Perhaps he was angry with her. Perhaps he was tired of her.

Perhaps he had found someone new. I am sure these were the kinds of thoughts she pondered as she considered Mordecai's request.

If she came unsolicited and he did not extend his scepter, the punishment was death. The king had already proven he was not afraid of disposing of a queen. Remember Vashti?

Prayer and fasting played a vital role in the salvation of the Jewish people. Esther (Church), we have just as urgent a situation today.

Living Up to Your Name

Esther, your name means "star." And do you know who the star represents? That is the name for Jesus in Revelation 22:16, "I am the ... bright and Morning STAR."

Every Jewish person has two names; one is from the culture in which he or she lives and the other is a Hebrew name. Esther, your Hebrew name is Hadassah, which means "myrtle." Myrtle is figurative of the gospel.

Esther, Hadassah, are you beginning to see your call based on your name? It is found in Philippians 2:15: "You shine like STARS [Esther] in the universe as you hold out the WORD OF LIFE [Gospel/Hadassah] ...."

Your name will become reality, Esther, when you begin to *fast and pray.*

Therefore Israel will be abandoned until the time when she who is in labor [Esther] gives birth ... (Mic. 5:3).

Esther, you will begin to give birth to spiritual children when you start fasting and travailing and are in labor.

... Yet no sooner is Zion in labor than she gives birth to her children (Is. 66:8).

It's Time to Go to the King

Suzette Hattingh, leader of intercession for the Reinhard Bonnke Ministries, says, "Prayer without evangelism is an arrow shot nowhere."[4] In other words, Esther, it is time to stand up for Israel and to reach out to the Jewish people with the gospel.

Today, God has the same message for you as He had in the book of Esther. You can be comfortable in your church, singing your hymns, having great fellowship and building golden cathedrals. But . . .

. . . Do not think that because you are in the king's house you alone of all the Jews will escape. For if you remain SILENT at this time, relief and deliverance for the Jews will arise from another place, but you and your father's family will PERISH. And who knows but that you have come to royal position for such a time as this? (Esth. 4:13-14)

Esther laid down her life and went to the king. And God gave her favor. The door to the king was very narrow. Esther's only way of entry was to be touched by the gold scepter. Today, the gold scepter for access to God (the King) is the Messiah.

4. As cited in Reinhard Bonnke, *Evangelism by Fire*, (London: Kingsway Publications, Ltd., 1989), p. 52.

9

The Fate of All Jew Haters

Satan missed out on Esther so he tried to destroy Mordecai. Satan used Haman's wife, Zeresh, to tell Haman to build a seventy-five foot gallows for Mordecai.

But then came the royal case of insomnia. Some would say the king's inability to sleep on this particular night was just a coincidence. But then how do you explain his desire to read the chronicles of the kingdom? And that he "just happened" to notice out of the thousands of pages the section about Mordecai saving his life? And that he "just happened" to ask what honor Mordecai received? And that Mordecai "just happened" to have received no reward? And that at the precise moment the king decides to reward Mordecai, Haman came to get permission to hang Mordecai?

There is a law of sowing and reaping, and Haman was about to get his due. Not only did he have to publicly honor Mordecai but he had a new problem — what to do with the seventy-five foot gallows. Then his wife had a revelation: ". . . Since Mordecai, before whom your downfall has started, is of Jewish origin, you cannot stand against him — you will surely come to ruin!" (Esth. 6:13).

But it was too late. Another law of God had taken effect. God uses Israel as His method of divine retribution. Israel is similar to Jesus, the "stone," in this respect. Remember when the Lord rebuked the Jewish leadership (not all the Jewish people), and quoted Psalm 118:22, "The STONE the builders rejected has become the chief capstone . . . "? And then He said, "He who falls on this stone will be broken to pieces [ouch, Haman!], but he on whom it falls will be crushed" (Matt. 21:44). God uses Israel the same way. Jeremiah 51:20 shows us what happens when someone touches the apple of God's eye, the Jew:

You [Israel] are my WAR CLUB, my WEAPON for battle — with you I shatter nations, with you I destroy kingdoms.

God can and has punished Israel, but anyone else who tries will be shattered. "All who devour you will be devoured . . ." (Jer. 30:16).

Haman's gallows were similar to satan's cross for Jesus. As Paul points out in 1 Corinthians 2:8:

None of the rulers of this age understood it, for if they had, they would not have crucified the Lord of glory.

If satan had understood, he never would have orchestrated the cross. It is the last thing he would have allowed because it spelled his defeat. And if Haman had realized who would swing on his gallows (type of cross), he never would have built them.

A New Weapon

At her second banquet for Haman and the king, Esther had the chutzpah (nerve) to reveal her Jewish connection and to plead for the lives of her people. As a result, the King changed his mind, but even he could not change his edict. There had to be a higher law to spare the Jewish people. The higher law was to allow them to defend themselves with the sword (Esth. 9:5). The sword is symbolic of the Word of God. When Jews today are equipped with the Word of God, they will not only defend themselves but will wreak havoc in the enemy's kingdom.

11

Haman and his ten sons and all the other enemies of the Jews were destroyed. God's word says, "No one could stand against them ..." (Esth. 9:2). People got so excited at the power displayed by these supposedly defenseless Jews that many Gentiles recognized that God was responsible, and revival broke out (Esth. 8:17).

Finally, the authority (the king's signet ring) was taken from Haman and given to Mordecai (Esth. 8:1, 2). The greatest lesson we learn from the book of Esther is found in the last verse:

Mordecai the Jew was second in rank to King Xerxes, preeminent among the Jews, and held in high esteem by his many fellow Jews, BECAUSE HE WORKED FOR THE GOOD OF HIS PEOPLE AND SPOKE UP FOR THE WELFARE OF ALL THE JEWS (Esth. 10:3).

CHAPTER TWO:

"EVERYTHING I HAVE IS YOURS"

ESTHER, YOU ARE THE OLDER BROTHER OF THE PRODIGAL SON. DO NOT BE JEALOUS OF THE ONE WHO HAS LEFT AND IS NOW RETURNING, FOR THE FATHER SAYS, "EVERYTHING I HAVE IS YOURS." ENDEAVOR TO BE REUNITED WITH THE JEWISH PEOPLE AS CHILDREN WITH THEIR FATHER AND AS MEMBERS OF THE SAME FLOCK WITH JESUS AS OUR SHEPHERD.

I Have Sinned

In the parable of the prodigal son, found in Luke 15:11-32, the younger son (physical Jew) took for granted his father, home and inheritance. He was a spoiled brat who thought the world owed him a living. After enjoying worldly pleasures and squandering his inheritance, he found himself in the pig sty, literally. For a Jew that had been taught all his life not to eat pork, this was his breaking-point. Things were so bad that he longed to eat the pigs' food but no one would let him. He felt he would surely die. Then he came to his senses. Maybe his father would forgive him. He had no excuses. He had no one to blame but himself. "Maybe my father would have enough mercy to let me work as one of his hired men," he thought.

So he made a decision:

I will set out and go back to my father and say to him: "Father, I HAVE SINNED against heaven and against you. I am no longer worthy to be called your son; make me like one of your hired men" (Luke 15:18, 19).

That simple decision and action brought about change way beyond anything he deserved or could even imagine. His father, instead of being angry, could not even see his sins anymore. He was so filled with compassion and joy that his son had come home that he ran instantly to him while he was a long way off and threw his arms around him and kissed him. He took away his soiled, tattered clothes and gave him his best clothing. Then he showed how complete his forgiveness was. He gave him his ring of author-ity. That meant that everything his father had was at his disposal. Listen to the gratefulness, joy and compassion in his father's words: "For this son of mine was dead and is alive again; he was lost and is found" (Luke 15:24).

The older brother (Gentile believer) was returning from the field when he heard the celebration. When he found out his good-for-nothing brother had come home and, worse yet, been accepted as if nothing were wrong, his anger got the best of him. He was so hurt he refused to attend the celebration. But his father found out and pleaded with him to not be jealous. "My son . . . you are always with me, and EVERYTHING I HAVE IS YOURS" (Luke 15:31).

Esther, you might be adopted, but your Father does not consider you a step-child. You have become a priest in His kingdom. You are royalty. He calls you his child. Not only is He no respecter of persons, but He says, "Everything I have is yours," and promises you will reign on the earth!

You were slain, and with your blood you purchased men for God from EVERY TRIBE AND LANGUAGE AND PEOPLE AND NATION. You have made them to be a KINGDOM AND PRIESTS to serve our God, and THEY WILL REIGN ON THE EARTH (Rev. 5:9, 10).

The Fathers and the Children

A friend, David Michael, shared a revelation with me from the last verses of the Old Testament. These verses are both chilling and mysterious:

See, I will send you the prophet Elijah before that great and dreadful day of the LORD comes. He will turn the hearts of the FATHERS TO THEIR CHILDREN, and the hearts of the CHILDREN TO THEIR FATHERS; OR ELSE I will come and strike the land with a CURSE (Mal. 4:5, 6).

Jesus is asked about this verse by His disciples. He says: ". . . To be sure, Elijah comes [literally, is going to come] and will restore all things" (Matt. 17:11). Then Jesus goes on to show how this was

15

partially fulfilled through the ministry of John the Baptist. But when He made this statement ("Elijah is going to come"), John had already been killed.

Malachi says the task of reconciliation between these two estranged groups must happen before the day of the Lord OR ELSE the world will suffer a CURSE. Who are these two estranged groups?

The "fathers" are associated with the JEWISH PEOPLE and the "children" are CHRISTIANS.

Both the Old and New Testament equate Judaism with "fathers." And the New Testament calls the followers of Jesus "children." Notice how Judaism is linked to the "fathers" in Romans 11:28:

> *As far as the gospel is concerned, they are enemies on your account; but as far as election is concerned, they are loved on account of the PATRIARCHS [FATHERS] . . .* [5]

One of many verses that refers to believers as children is Hebrews 2:13. This passage pictures Jesus saying, "Here am I, and the CHILDREN God has given me." (Also, note Gal. 3:7, 26; 4:27, 28; and Luke 3:8.) According to Malachi, the consequence of the breach between the fathers and the children is for the earth to be struck with a curse.

5. Other references to this connection include: John 7:22; Is. 51:1,2; and Luke 1:55. (For further illustrations of Jesus' relationship to the faith of the Israelite fathers, see Acts 3:13, 25; 5:30, 31; 13: 17, 32, 33; Luke 1:32, 33.)

The connection between respect for parents and a curse is also found in the Ten Commandments:

Honor your father and your mother, as the LORD your God has commanded you, so that you may LIVE LONG and that it may GO WELL WITH YOU . . . (Deut. 5:16).

Who are the "parents" of Christianity? To whom do we trace our heritage and roots? Paul pleads with us in Romans 9:2-5 not to forget the debt we owe those who paved the way for us:

I have great sorrow and unceasing anguish in my heart. For I could wish that I myself were cursed and cut off from [Messiah] for the sake of my brothers, those of my own race, the people of Israel. Theirs is the adoption as sons, theirs the divine glory, the covenants, the receiving of the law, the temple worship and the promises. Theirs are the patriarchs, and from them is traced the human ancestry of [Messiah] . . . .

One Flock, One Shepherd

Here is the conclusion: *God is going to turn the hearts of the Jews to the Christians and the hearts of the Christians to the Jews.*

God is interested in these two people being one. Jesus makes this clear to his Jewish followers in John 10:16:

I have other sheep that are not of this sheep pen. I must bring them also. They too will listen to my voice, and there shall be ONE FLOCK and ONE SHEPHERD.

17

Since the heart of God is to make Christians and Jews one in Jesus, can you see why the devil has tried to make us distrust each other?

CHAPTER THREE:

BEATING SATAN'S STRATEGY

ESTHER, GOD HAS NOT GIVEN YOU A SPIRIT OF FEAR. YOU ARE ABOUT TO ENTER INTO AN ARENA THAT WILL MAKE YOU THE GREATEST IN THE KINGDOM OF HEAVEN!

Your Family Just Expanded

Power got into the wrong hands in the book of Esther. Haman, an anti-messiah type, got the king's signet ring. When he used this seal to authorize an order, no one could reverse it. The situation looked impossible for the Jewish people. But God was not about to let His people down; His reputation rested on their survival. And His plan for their survival required humans to pray and fast.

19

For whom do you pray first, others or your immediate family? Do you believe the words of Galatians 3:29? "If you belong to [Messiah], then you are Abraham's seed, and heirs according to the promise." If you have the blessings of Abraham, then you also have the responsibilities. Guess what, Church? Your immediate family has just expanded. Consider every Jewish person you meet as immediate family. And pray for them as you would a mother, father, brother, sister, wife, husband or child!

The Real Thing

To pray effectively, we need to know the enemy's moves in advance. The devil's strategy is rather simple. First, he gets the Jewish person to turn away from established religion. For a year I prayed in a traditional synagogue and three times a week we prayed a prayer from the prayer book for the sick. I never heard one report of answered prayer. If I were a traditional Jew today, I too might question the reality of a personal God.

After the devil gets the Jew away from his traditional beliefs, he attempts to fill the spiritual void with the occult or cult groups. This is fairly easy because Jews are the only people identified in the Bible with a built-in zeal for God, "but their zeal is not based on knowledge" (Rom. 10:2).

When in Miami Beach several years ago, I spoke with a member of the Hari Krishna Movement whose group had just purchased a hotel on the boardwalk. She said the majority of their followers in the hotel were Jewish and that there was a high percentage of Jews in their organization throughout the United States.

Ron Cohen, a Messianic Jew, and previously a practicing Yogi, estimates that up to 70 percent of the practicing Yogis in America are Jewish. Israel has more Transcendental Meditation practitioners per capita than any other country. The majority of the Jews I have interviewed over the past fifteen years who have accepted Jesus were previously in the occult. Their experience shows a large number of Jews in all the occult and cult groups.

Jewish people make up only one quarter of one percent of the world's population. If satan is not specifically targeting the Jews, why such a high percentage in cults and the occult? Another question to ponder: If Jews are so open to the counterfeit, what will happen when they are exposed to the real thing?

Fear of Sharing Jesus

That leads to the next tactic of the devil — preventing Jews from being exposed to the truth. Most Christians are afraid to witness to Jewish people. Some are afraid they will ruin their wonderful friendships. Some are enamored by their acceptance in the Jewish community and prefer just to preach a gospel of blessing Israel. Some are afraid they do not know enough about the Old Testament. Some think God has a special plan of salvation for the Jew. I even met one group of Christians who said Jews were not going to be saved until after the rapture, so why bother witnessing to them? I wanted to shout, "But what about those who die before the rapture?!"

Peter answered most of these objections in Acts 4:12:

Salvation is found in no one else, for there is NO OTHER NAME UNDER HEAVEN GIVEN TO MEN BY WHICH WE MUST BE SAVED.

By the time you finish this book you will know more of the biblical facts about the Messiah than 99% of the rabbis. And, remember, the average Jewish person knows very little about the Old Testament.

Please forgive me for how hard the next two questions sound, but I must ask them. Are you more interested in what people think about you than whether they end up in hell? Do you value your relationships with your Jewish friends more than where they will spend eternity?

The Most Dangerous Man in America

Friendship evangelism is the best kind of evangelism. I am convinced the most love-starved people on the face of this earth are the Jewish people. As you walk in unconditional love, you will earn the right to share the Messiah. Esther, your call is written: "Salvation has come to the Gentiles to make Israel envious" (Rom. 11:11). You have been saved for a major assignment from God... "to make Israel envious."

In a recent interview, Dr. Frank Eiklor told me what happened when a Jewish temple in Fullerton, California was set on fire by an unknown anti-Semitic group and three of the temple's members were threatened with death. Dr. Eiklor, along with other prominent Christians, called a press conference and said: "We want to let you

22

know, open season on the Jews has been closed. Any attack against the Jewish people will be considered an attack against our churches and persons. We Christians make Jewish pain our own!"

Then, since talk is cheap, the local Christians repaired the temple. Dr. Eiklor demonstrated to the rabbi as well as the entire Jewish community that he loved them unconditionally. He would show them this love even if they never accepted Jesus!

One Jewish leader told Dr. Eiklor, "Eiklor, you're the most dangerous man to us in America." Then he smiled and said, "If more Christians would treat us like you do, you'd remove our best excuses for saying that Jesus isn't real."

Who Shall Be the Greatest?

Isaiah 49:22-23 contains another hard teaching for Esther. (Perhaps we have to soak a little longer in the myrrh and perfume.) This directive by God is similar to Jesus' act of washing the disciples' feet.

> *See, I will beckon to the Gentiles, I will lift up my banner to the peoples; they will bring your sons in their arms and carry your daughters on their shoulders. Kings will be your foster fathers, and their queens your nursing mothers. They will bow down before you with their faces to the ground; they will lick the dust at your feet.*

Esther, if you do this, satan is through. Look at the end of the verse: ". . . Then you [the Jewish people] will know that I am the Lord . . . ." And you, Esther, will be the GREATEST IN THE KINGDOM OF HEAVEN.

Whoever wants to become GREAT among you must be your servant . . . (Matt. 20:26).

The GREATEST among you should be like the youngest, and the one who rules like the one who serves . . . (Luke 22:26).

Esther had a choice: to try to protect her position as queen on earth or to be greatest in heaven. She realized the books are not completely settled in this life. There is a heavenly balancing that happens when this experience called life, this blink of the eye, compared to eternity, is finished. Paul so loved the Jewish people he was willing to give up his eternal life for them (Rom. 9:3). Esther so loved the Jews she was willing to give up her life as queen for them. And Jesus so loved the world that He gave up His life for all who would receive Him.

What are you willing to give up?

CHAPTER FOUR:

WARPED THEOLOGY: A TRAGIC HERITAGE

ESTHER, YOU HAVE A PAST THAT MANY HAVE BEEN IGNORANT OF AND OTHERS HAVE EVEN TRIED TO HIDE. BUT, ESTHER, YOU ARE ABOUT TO LEARN WHAT HURTS THE JEWISH PEOPLE. THIS WILL HELP YOU NEVER TO BE PARTY TO THE SAME MISTAKE.

Trouble in the Family

Who can hurt you the most? Can a complete stranger get to you as much as a member of your immediate family? Jews and Christians are from the same family. We have the same God. A Jew is the physical seed of Abraham; a Christian the spiritual seed. We believe in and accept the same Holy Scriptures. All the events described in all the Gospels, except for a short visit to Egypt by

Joseph, Mary and Jesus, took place in a Jewish land, Israel. Every one of the New Testament authors was Jewish, except Luke, and he was a proselyte to Judaism. Jews and Christians are forever connected by deep mishpocha (family) relationships.[6] And yet, there is trouble in the family.

How has the devil managed to build such distrust between close family members? Primarily through his very nature — lying. The big lie did not start with Hitler, but the devil. A warped understanding of theology taught by the early Church said the Jews were solely responsible for the crucifixion of Jesus. Few Christians are aware of the horrors inflicted on the Jewish community because of this teaching. If only they had read the Scriptures and THOUGHT FOR THEMSELVES. Jesus put it this way: "If a blind man leads a blind man, both will fall into a pit" (Matt. 15:14).

For the record, God tells us who killed Jesus in Acts 4:27:

Indeed HEROD and PONTIUS PILATE met together with the GENTILES and the PEOPLE OF ISRAEL in this city to conspire against your holy servant Jesus . . . .

So who killed Jesus? When you get the Jews and Gentiles together you have the whole world. And yet even the whole world could not have killed Jesus unless it was part of God's plan. The Scriptures say: "For GOD so loved the WORLD that HE GAVE his one and only son . . . " (John 3:16). And Jesus said, ". . . I LAY DOWN MY LIFE for the sheep" (John 10:15). No one person or people group killed Jesus; He laid down His life voluntarily, as the

6. If you want to know what great event is going to happen next in the church, watch natural Israel. God always moves first with natural Israel, then with the spiritual seed of Abraham.

Passover Lamb that takes away the sins of the world. Jesus died because of sin, not because of Jews.

"Christian" Anti-Semitism

The second major strategy to divide Jews and Christians was introduced by an influential early Church leader, Origen of Alexandria (A.D. 185-254). He was the first to interpret all Scripture allegorically rather than literally. Certainly there are biblical passages that have an allegorical meaning. However, this method of interpretation *replaces* the literal meaning with an allegorical one. It claims that the Israelites permanently lost all their blessings and calling by rejecting Jesus as the Messiah. These covenants now belong only to the Church — the "new Israel." Then it goes on to say the Jews have no future as a chosen people.

Through the centuries, accusations and statements by Church leaders against the Jews have led to a vicious form of Christian anti-Semitism. Here are a few examples:[7]

Justin Martyr *(d. A.D.167) was one of the first to accuse the Jews of inciting to kill Christians.*

Origen *(d. A.D.254) accused Jews of plotting in their meetings to murder Christians.*

Author Malcolm Hay writes: "When Origen wrote at the beginning of the fourth century that 'the Jews . . . nailed Christ to the cross' (De Principüs, IV, 8), he . . . may have meant

7. Unless otherwise noted, the following historical references are from Steffi Rubin, *Anti-Semitism* (Copyright Hineni Ministries, 1977), pp. 32-33.

something different from what he said — but for many centuries his words were taken as literally true by all Christendom." [8]

Eusebius *(c. A.D. 300) alleged that Jews, each year at the holiday of Purim engaged in ceremonial killing of Christian children.*

St. Hilary of Poitiers *(d. A.D. 367) said that the Jews were a perverse people, forever accursed by God.*

St. Ephraem *(d. A.D. 373) wrote many of the early Church hymns, some of which maligned Jews, even to the point of calling the Jewish synagogues "whore-houses."*

St. John Chrysostom *(A.D. 344-407) said that there could never be expiation for the Jews and that God had always hated them. He said it was "incumbent" on all Christians to hate the Jews. The Jews were assassins of Christ, and worshippers of the devil.*

Malcolm Hay writes: "The violence of the language used by St. John Chrysostom in his homilies against the Jews has never been exceeded by any preacher whose sermons have been recorded." [9]

In one of these homilies, St. John Chrysostom stated: "The synagogue is worse than a brothel . . . it is a den of scoundrels and the repair of wild beasts . . . the temple of demons devoted to idolatrous cults . . . the refuge of brigands and debauchees, and the cavern of devils." [10]

8. X. Malcolm Hay, *Europe and the Jews* (Boston, Beacon Press, 1961), p. 16.

9. Hay, p. 27.

10. As cited in Hay, pp. 27-28.

St. Cyril *(d. A.D. 444), gave the Jews within his jurisdiction the choice of conversion, exile or stoning.*

St. Jerome *(d. A.D. 420), translator of the Latin Vulgate, "proved" that Jews are incapable of understanding the Scriptures, and that they should be severely persecuted until they confess the "true faith."*

St. Augustine *(d. A.D. 430) called Judaism a corruption. The true image of the Jew, he said, was Judas Iscariot, forever guilty and ignorant spiritually. Augustine decided that Jews, for their own good and the good of society, must be relegated to the position of slaves. This theme was later picked up by St. Thomas Aquinas (d. A.D. 1274), who demanded that Jews be called to perpetual servitude.*

According to Professor F. E. Talmage, St. Augustine believed that "because of their sin against Christ, the Jews rightly deserved death. Yet, as with Cain who murdered the just Abel, they are not to die . . . . For they are doomed to wander the earth . . . the 'witnesses of their iniquity and of our truth,' the living proof of Christianity." [11]

Crusaders *(A.D. 1099) rounded up all the Jews into the Great Synagogue in Jerusalem. When they were securely inside the locked doors, the synagogue was set afire. And the misguided Crusaders, with the lies of perverted sermons fresh in their ears, sang as they marched around the blaze, "Christ, we adore Thee."*

11. F. E. Talmage, ed., *Disputation and Dialgogue: Readings in the Jewish-Christian Encounter* (New York: Ktav Publishing House, Inc., 1975), P. 18.

Martin Luther *(c. 1544) added fuel to the fire by saying that the Jews should not merely be slaves, but slaves of slaves, that they might not even come into contact with Christians. In his "Schem Hamphoras," he said the Jews were ritual murderers, poisoners of wells; he called for all Talmuds and synagogues to be destroyed.*

In his "Von den Juden und Iren Luegen" (1543), Luther writes: "What then shall we Christians do with this damned, rejected race of Jews? Since they live among us and we know about their lying and blasphemy and cursing, we cannot tolerate them if we do not wish to share in their lies, curses, and blasphemy.... We must prayerfully and reverentially practice a merciful severity." [12]

Some may question why I am rehashing this sad history. Let me quote from the Encyclopedia Judaica as it comments on Martin Luther's statements: "Short of the Auschwitz oven and extermination, the whole Nazi Holocaust is pre-outlined here." [13] Adolph Hitler wrote in *Mein Kampf,* "Hence today I believe that I am acting in accordance with the Almighty Creator: by defending myself against the JEW, I am fighting for the work of the Lord." [14]

We Jewish people know of these poisoned words written by Christian leaders. And worse, our enemies know these words and have used them to kill us. Most Jewish people have lost one or more

12. As cited in *Encyclopaedia Judaica* (Jerusalem: Keter Publishing House Jerusalem Ltd., 1972), Vol. 8, p. 692.

13. *Encyclopaedia Judaica*, Vol. 8, p. 693.

14. Adolf Hitler, *Mein Kampf,* translated by Ralph Manheim (Boston: Houghton Mifflin Co. 1971), p. 65.

relatives to anti-Semitism. Rose Price, a Holocaust survivor, lost nearly all of her family to the Nazis. When she entered the concentration camp, on the archway it read, "We kill you because you killed Jesus." When she got out, she wanted to burn churches.[15] I am not excusing this, but can you blame her? What would you have done in her situation?

When I was sharing the Messiah with several of my own relatives that survived the Holocaust, they could not hear my Good News because they were so filled with hurt and anger toward God and Christianity. One cousin told of S.S. troops (elite Nazi officers) that ripped her infant son from her arms and threw him out the window to the cement pavement from a second-floor apartment. When I pleaded with them that these were not true Christians, my cousin said: "The belt buckle of the S.S., read, 'In God We Trust.' " Try to proclaim the Gospel to some of my family members . . .

Confronting My Sister's Murderer

Only the love that God gives can cut through all the sad history of Christian anti-Semitism. Corrie ten Boom saw her father and sister suffer agonizing deaths because they chose to hide Jewish people from the Nazis. One day, many years after the war, Corrie recognized a guard from the concentration camp where she and her sister had been sent for hiding Jews from the Nazis. The guard was in the audience at a church where Corrie was speaking. He came forward and said, "You mentioned Ravensbruck in your talk. I was a guard there. But since that time," he went on, "I have become a Christian. I know that God has forgiven me for the cruel

15. From an interview with Rose Price on Messianic Vision radio broadcast #21 (broadcast June 1977).

things I did there, but I would like to hear it from your lips as well. Fraulein . . . will you forgive me?"[16]

What would she do? What would you do to someone who brutalized and killed your sister? What would Jesus do? It would be difficult, if not impossible, to forgive him in your natural strength. As Corrie "willed" to forgive him, the love of God shot like an electric current through her body, bringing tears to her eyes. "I forgive you, brother!" she cried.[17]

Remember Rose Price, the Jewish woman who had wanted to burn down churches because she thought Christians were responsible for killing her family? One day, the love of God reached through all that hurt and anger and she made Jesus Lord. Many years later, she was invited to Germany to share her testimony. She had promised herself she would never go back to the land that had spilled so much Jewish blood. But the love of God compelled her to go to Berlin. In the same stadium where Hitler swore the master race would rule for 1,000 years, she told the German Christian audience, "I forgive you." The stadium was draped with Israeli flags, German youths had Stars of David around their necks,[18] and several former S.S. guards ran up with tears in their eyes asking for

16. Corrie ten Boom, "I'm Still Learning to Forgive," Reprint from *Guideposts Magazine,* Copyright 1972 by Guideposts Associates, Inc., Carmel, New York 10512.

17. Ibid

18. Some Christians refuse to wear the Star of David because a six-pointed star is used in witchcraft. Did you know a five-pointed star is also used, as well as portions of Scripture? These same misguided Christians have a double standard. I don't see them refusing to fly (Cont.)

forgiveness. Jesus said: ". . . Everything is possible for him who believes" (Mark 9:23).

(Cont.) American flags (five-pointed stars) or cutting out passages from their Bibles. Just because the devil uses our precious symbols and Scriptures, should we bow to him? The Star of David is the most "Christian" jewelry you can wear. It identifies you with the Jewish people. And when a Jew says to you a non-Jew, "Why are you wearing a Jewish Star?" you can say, "because I have come to love the greatest Jew Who ever lived!" Now you are truly provoking the Jew to jealousy.

CHAPTER FIVE:

TRUTH AND CONSEQUENCES

ESTHER, WHO IS BETTER EQUIPPED TO DEFEND THE JEWISH PEOPLE THAN YOU? BUT, ESTHER, YOU MUST KNOW THE TRUTH — SIGNS OF HOLO- CAUST II ARE UPON US!

Today, world opinion is turning increasingly against the Jew due to the Palestinian protests and riots in Israel. Just a short time ago, Israel was the "David" and the Palestinians the "Goliath." But now the roles are reversed.

Who is right? What are the facts?

The problem in the Middle East is not a political problem and cannot be solved by politicians. The problem is spiritual and can only be settled by applying God's Word. Our position must line up with God's Word. God was the first Zionist. A Zionist believes the Jewish people are granted the right to the land of Israel forever.

God's Promises to Israel

GOD GIVES THE LAND TO THE JEWISH PEOPLE FOREVER.

> *The LORD said to Abram . . . . All the land that you see I will give to you and your offspring FOREVER* (Gen. 13:14, 15).

EVEN THE EXACT BOUNDARIES ARE SPELLED OUT.

> *On that day the LORD made a covenant with Abram and said, 'To your descendants I give this land, from the river of Egypt to the great river, the Euphrates — the land of the Kenites, Kenizzites, Kadmonites, Hittites, Perizzites, Rephaites, Amorites, Canaanites, Girgashites and Jebusites'* (Gen. 15:18-21).

CONDITIONAL COVENANTS REQUIRE TWO OR MORE PEOPLE PASSING BETWEEN THE SACRIFICE. THIS ONE ONLY HAS ONE (GOD) AND IS AN UNCONDITIONAL COVENANT.

> *A blazing torch [God] appeared and passed between the pieces. On that day the LORD made a covenant with Abram and said, 'To your descendants I give this land . . . '* (Gen. 15:17, 18).

36

WAS THE LAND GIVEN TO ISHMAEL (THE FATHER OF THE ARABS), ABRAHAM'S OTHER SON?

> *Then God said, 'Yes, but your wife Sarah will bear you a son, and you will call him ISAAC. I will establish my covenant with him as an EVERLASTING covenant for his descendants after him. And as for ISHMAEL, I have heard you: I will surely bless him . . . . But MY COVENANT I WILL ESTABLISH WITH ISAAC . . .' (Gen. 17:19-21).*

GOD SUMMARIZES HIS LAND COVENANT AGAIN.

> *He remembers his covenant forever, the word he commanded, for a thousand generations [40,000 years], the covenant he made with Abraham, the oath he swore with Isaac. He confirmed it to Jacob as a decree, to Israel as an everlasting covenant: To you I will give the land of Canaan [Israel] as the portion you will inherit (Ps. 105:8-11).*

It is important to emphasize that to be pro-Jewish is not to be anti-Arab — God loves both cousins. And when the Israelis do something wrong, they should be confronted. BUT WHEN IT COMES TO THE LAND, I MUST TAKE GOD'S POSITION.

Spiritualizing the Promises

The only way satan can undermine the absolute position of God on this critical issue is to spiritualize the promises to the Jew and Israel and say God replaced them with His new people, the Church.

37

This is called Replacement Theology and is spreading rapidly throughout Christianity.[19]

I am in favor of finding spiritual application to the Word of God as is clearly evidenced in this book. However, it is not necessary to exclude the literal meaning of God's Word at the same time. Every time satan has managed to undermine the literal integrity of God's Word, those involved go into heresy. Let us allow God to speak for Himself.

FIRST, HE ADDRESSES THIS NEWLY RESURGED MOVEMENT.

> *Have you not noticed that these people are saying, "The LORD has rejected the two kingdoms [Judea and Israel] he chose"? So they despise my people and no longer regard them as a nation. This is what the LORD says: "If I have not established my covenant with day and night and the fixed laws of heaven and earth, then I will reject the descendants of Jacob and David my servant . . . . For I will restore their fortunes and have compassion on them"* (Jer. 33:24-26).

> *I ask then: Did God reject his people? By no means!* (Rom. 11:1).

LET US SUBSTITUTE "ISRAEL" FOR "THE CHURCH" AS THEY SUGGEST.

19. For an in-depth analysis of Replacement Theology see Part IV, "Is the Church the 'New Israel'?" by Keith Parker.

... because of [the CHURCH'S] transgression, salvation has come to the Gentiles to make [the CHURCH] envious. But if [the CHURCH'S] transgression means riches for the world, and [its] loss means riches for the Gentiles, how much greater riches will [its] fullness bring! ... As far as the gospel is concerned, [the MEMBERS OF THE CHURCH] are enemies on your account; but as far as election is concerned, they are loved on account of the patriarchs, for God's gifts and his call are irrevocable (Rom. 11:11-12, 28-29).

Did salvation come to the Gentiles because the Church rejected it? Was it riches for the Gentiles because of the Church's transgression? Is the Church God's enemy? Is the Church loved because of the promises made to Abraham, Isaac and Jacob (the Patriarchs)? And if God rejected Israel for disobedience, what chance does the Church or anyone have if God is so fickle and changes His mind? God's Word says, "God's gifts and his call are IRREVOCABLE" (Rom. 11:29). If you can trust God with His promises to the physical seed of Abraham, you can trust Him with His promises to the spiritual seed of Abraham.

But what about Galatians 3:28, which states: "There is neither Jew nor Greek, slave nor free, male nor female, for you are all one in [Messiah] Jesus"? Last time I looked, we still had males and females. Paul is obviously saying that in the Spirit there is no distinction, but in the flesh there are gifts and callings and responsibilities. Even the behavior of husbands and wives is clearly stated in Scripture.

Spiritualizing the promises inevitably leads to anti-Semitism. In a recent message, one of the leaders in the Replacement

Theology movement said, "The Kingdom has been taken over from Israel, and it has been possessed by the New Covenant People. Israel has become demon possessed." [20]

A noted author, in a book that presents the premise that the Church alone is Israel, goes so far as to state that the Ashkenazic Jews (Jews of Eastern Europe) are not Jews. [21] He says all Ashkenazic Jews are descended from the Khazars. And he claims the Khazars were not Jews because they converted to Judaism. This is a "big lie." Does this make King David a non-Jew? David had two converts to Judaism in his background — Ruth and Rahab! Also, since God said the Jews would be persecuted and in the last days would return to their land, isn't it strange that He would do this with people who are not Jews! The author goes against history, logic and truth with his thesis. [Incidentally, those who say Jews are only from the tribe of Judah have not read Esther. Mordecai of the tribe of Benjamin was called a Jew (Esth. 2:5).]

Also, this author quotes from the Talmud words misconstrued or pulled out of context that will be used to try to turn the Church anti-Jewish and anti-Israel — fuel for the next Hitler. Perhaps the best example of this is where he claims that the Talmud says it is permissible for a priest to have sex with or marry a girl who is three years and one day old. What the Talmud is actually referring to is that, in the case of a *woman* who became a *proselyte to Judaism*

20. As cited in Hal Lindsey, *The Road to Holocaust* (New York: Bantam Books, 1989), p. 25.

21. I have deliberately omitted the name of this author and his book. He is a fine Christian who I'm sure never intended for his statements to be used to support anti-Semitism.

before the age of three years and one day, she may, *as an adult*, be considered a true Israelite, and therefore eligible to marry a priest. Judaism would never approve of the situation insinuated by the author! Each of his other examples reflects a misunderstanding of the Talmud.

Please understand that, although the Talmud is a highly moral collection of laws, I am not defending it as the inspired Word of God; it is the work of man and includes many unbiblical opinions and practices that we must reject. For instance, there are several obscure references against Jesus. However, we should not allow to go unchallenged blatant lies about the beliefs of Judaism that serve no other purpose than to incite people to hate Jews.

The book I have described is riddled with error, but those who are ignorant of Hebrew, Judaism and the Talmud will be deceived by its titillating lies. I would like to ask those investing their lives in this lie of Christian anti-Semitism the following questions: If God is through with the Jews and Israel, why did He say . . .

1)   . . . He would make Israel a great nation? (Gen. 12:2)

2)   . . . He would scatter the Jewish people from their home-land? (Deut. 28:36, 37)

3)   . . . He would reestablish the nation of Israel and regather the Jews home? (Jer. 16:15)

4)   . . . the Jews would return to Israel in unbelief and then He would reveal Himself when they are restored to the land? (Ezek. 36:24, 25)

41

5)   . . . a major goal of the Church was to reach Jews with the gospel? (Rom. 11:11)

6)   . . . that people would say the Lord has rejected Israel? (Jer. 33:24-26)

7)   . . . it would be greater riches for the Gentiles when the Jews are saved? (Rom. 11:12)

8)   . . . all Israel will be saved? (Rom. 11:26)

If God is through with Israel, why did he predict Israel's future, write about it in the Bible and have it come true with 100% accuracy? If He honored His Word literally in the Old Testament, why would He not do it in the New?

As a logical student of God's Word, it makes no sense to ignore the Scriptures I have mentioned. But many have. And many more will. The consequences of doing so will be disastrous — particularly in the political arena.

An End-Time Scenario

Consider this scenario. Jewish groups begin to feel threatened by increasingly vocal and politically active religious groups who deny that God still has a calling on the Jewish people. "Take the kingdom by force," these militant politicians say. The Jews are not opposed to Christian symbols or any other religious symbols. However, to them, a manger scene on public property or mandatory school prayer appears to be the first step toward undermining the religious freedom of Jews. They remember all too well the anti-Semitism perpetuated throughout history by "Christians" in the name of the cross. Since Replacement Theology proclaims that

42

God is through with the Jews, guess who people begin to think of as the enemy of God? Sound familiar? Remember the words of Adolph Hitler in Mein Kampf, " . . . by defending myself against the JEW, I am fighting for the work of the Lord."

The occult quietly becomes respectable. Many scientists build elaborate scenarios to prove that mind control, hallucinatory drugs, and crystals heal the body. Their ideas are taught in elementary schools and gain great acceptability. Doctors begin to use these occult techniques as part of their normal practice. Christian ministers begin to say it was wrong to reject the spiritual knowledge that the East has known for thousands of years. And 1 Timothy 4:1 comes to pass: "The Spirit clearly says that in later times some will abandon the faith and follow deceiving spirits and things taught by demons."

The United States, enamored with the Soviet Union, sends it large sums of money. This is possible because, although America's debt is at an all-time high, investors like the Japanese and the Arabs are investing large sums of money in the U.S. However, suddenly the foreign investment stops as investors find the new United States of Europe more attractive.

About the same time, the American stock market collapses. When Japan suffered a similar calamity a few years ago, the Jews were blamed — even though there are very few Jews in the entire country.[22] *What could happen in America with the world's largest Jewish population?*

22. Eighty-six anti-Semitic books have been published in Japan in the 18-month period prior to February 1990. They blame Japan's financial woes on a Jewish money conspiracy (Simon Wiesenthal Center Newsletter, February 1, 1990).

The crash triggers the closing of banks, and retirement programs cannot pay benefits. Farms go bankrupt, food is rationed and many are homeless. Drugs, AIDS and crime rage out of control. Race riots erupt. About this time an old book called "The Protocols of The Elders of Zion" resurfaces. This book blames the Jews for the woes of the world. Anti-Semitic hate groups, many with Christian names, begin to recruit record numbers of people.

Meanwhile, Christians have been voting in politicians that stand for biblical "right." They are not Christians but cater to the powerful Christian vote. Strange coalitions have been formed for the sake of political expediency. Things are so bad the politicians need a scapegoat . . .

Remember, this is only a scenario. However, there is Scripture that indicates something will cause the Jews to flee the West (America): ". . . When he [the Lord] roars, his children will come TREMBLING from the WEST" (Hos. 11:10). Also, Jeremiah 16:15 says God will bring up the Jews "out of ALL the countries where he had banished them."

If this came to pass in a similar fashion to the scenario, whose side would you be on, Esther? Today, it is not life-threatening to be pro-Jewish or pro-Israel. What if it were to cost you your life or the life of a family member? After all, no one knows of your roots. No one knows the JEWISH MESSIAH lives inside of you. You have hidden your roots and heritage well. Remember, Esther in the Bible was also told to hide her Jewish roots. God was maneuvering His queen into a position of authority "for such a time as this" (Esth. 4:14).

Potential Holocaust?

When I was in Israel, I interviewed the assistant director of an unusual museum — "The Museum for the Potential Holocaust" located in Jerusalem. It is filled with magazines and newspapers, most of them from the United States, that promote anti-Semitism. Sadly, most of this anti-Jewish literature contains Christian words and symbols. Satan is up to his old tricks — to make Jews distrust Christians.

I asked the Director, "Do you believe there could be another Holocaust in the United States?"

"Yes," she replied.

Then I said, "There are many Christians that love the Jewish people. Do you think if there were another Holocaust they would stand up for the Jews?"

She looked at me, then pensively looked up toward the ceiling and said, "I don't know. I just don't know."

CHAPTER SIX:

THE LAW OF EVANGELISM

ESTHER, WHEN YOU REACH OUT TO THE JEW, YOU OPEN A SUPERNATURAL DOOR OF BLESSING TO REACH MYRIADS OF GENTILES WITH THE GOOD NEWS.

Hell Is Real

The German evangelist Reinhard Bonnke has said: "I want to plunder hell to populate heaven." Hell is real and was never intended for humans. I interviewed a godly grandmother whom Jesus took to hell to report to the world of its reality. I asked Mary Kathryn Baxter to describe the worst thing she observed. She said it was the time Jesus said to her, "I'm going to leave you here to experience hell without Me." [23]

Words cannot describe the feelings she experienced. No human on this earth has ever been separated from the love of God. Hell has only darkness, death and despair. The pain is real. You have all your memories of the times you rejected God. And the worst part is you know there is no chance of forgiveness or pardon. You will stay in that state of horror, torment, loneliness and darkness forever!

The apathy that surrounds most Christians when they have opportunity to witness makes me think they do not believe in hell. Yet, I know better. They have succumbed to twentieth-century American Christianity. Their excuses are numerous: My friends are not witnessing so why should I? Witnessing is the job of an evangelist. I have a different ministry . . . etc., etc., etc.

These Christians ignore what Jesus said in Mark 16:15: ". . . Go into all the world and preach the good news to all creation." In response to Jesus' command, ". . . the DISCIPLES went out and preached everywhere . . ." (v. 20).

Are you a disciple of Jesus? Then put aside your excuses and obey the words of Jesus. Your job is not to win anyone to the Lord. Your orders are to tell people the gospel in love. Only the Holy Spirit can take your words and make Jesus real. BUT HE NEEDS YOUR WORDS.

23. From an interview with Mary Kathryn Baxter on Messianic Vision radio broadcast #613 (broadcast July 1989).

To the Jew First . . .

Another mystery that is revealed in the book of Esther is the law of evangelism. It is supernatural and can only come to us from the Word of God.

Esther 8:17 says, "And many people of other nationalities became Jews because fear of the Jews had seized them." When Esther stood up for the Jewish people, revival broke out among the Gentiles.

This pattern for evangelism was described by Paul in Romans 1:16:

I am not ashamed of the gospel, because it is the power of God for the salvation of everyone who believes: FIRST FOR THE JEW, then for the Gentile.

This is not only the historical order for evangelism but the spiritual order. Paul, who was an evangelist to the Gentiles, always went to the Jew first.

The seed of this law is found in Genesis 12:3. God promises to bless those who bless the Jewish people. What is the greatest blessing you have ever received? Most likely you would say your salvation. What is the greatest blessing you can give the Jewish people? Salvation. This seed planted in Jewish evangelism will be multiplied in a harvest of Gentile evangelism.

Zechariah (8:23) tells us that in the last days

. . . ten men from all languages and nations will take firm hold of one Jew by the hem of his robe and say, 'Let us go with you, because we have heard that GOD IS WITH YOU.'

In verse 22, Zechariah tells us Israel will be the center of revival in the last days and many Gentiles and powerful nations will come to Jerusalem to seek the Lord. The world will be turned upside down when God raises up 144,000 end-time Jewish evangelists who live only for the Lamb (Rev. 14:1)! Multitudes of Gentiles will be swept into the kingdom by the ministry of these fiery Jewish evangelists (Rev. 7:9).

The law of evangelism is also demonstrated in the book of Jonah. Jonah was a type of the Jewish people. When he disobeyed the call of God, he was thrown into the sea. This symbolizes the Jewish people being thrown to the nations (the four corners of the earth). While in the sea (nations), he was miraculously preserved. The big fish represents Babylon. Jonah was stuck in Babylon and the only way he would fulfill his call was to be "vomited" out. When Jonah returned, repentance and salvation came to the Gentiles.

The World's Greatest Revival

The word "Jew" means a praiser of God. Although many Jews and Christians say we should not proselytize, how can you be a true Jew (praiser of God) unless you declare His majesty, mercy and grace to everyone? Isaiah (66:19) tells us that in the last days Israel will fulfill her priestly call.

I will set a sign among them, and I will send some of those who survive [from Israel] to the nations . . . and to the distant islands that have not heard of my fame or seen my glory. THEY WILL PROCLAIM MY GLORY AMONG THE NATIONS.

In Acts 2:17-21, Peter quotes Joel and explains what the Jewish people have just seen and heard at Pentecost (Shavuot). However, Peter stops without finishing the prophecy from Joel. With God's time clock now running on "rapid time" since the release of the Jews from Russia, it is time for the rest of the prophecy to come to pass:

> . . . *for on Mount Zion and in Jerusalem there will be deliverance, as the LORD has said, among the survivors whom the Lord calls* (Joel 3:32).

Who are the survivors (remnant) living in Jerusalem that will proclaim deliverance to the world? They are the Jews who survived 2,000 years of banishment and have returned to Israel.

Now you are beginning to see why satan has used and will continue to use humans to try to destroy the Jewish people. When Esther (the Church) starts going to the Jew first, REVIVAL WILL BREAK OUT AMONG THE GENTILES. This is what Paul is describing in Romans 11:12 when he says,

> *But if their transgression means riches for the world, and their loss means riches for the Gentiles, HOW MUCH GREATER RICHES WILL THEIR FULLNESS BRING!*

CHAPTER SEVEN:

FULLNESS OF GENTILES

ESTHER, OPEN YOUR EYES. WE ARE AT THE CLOSE OF THE AGE. AND YOUR PART IN JEWISH REVIVAL WILL USHER IN THE KING!

A Mystery Revealed

God is in the process of restoring truth and revealing mysteries to the Church. Paul calls Israel a "mystery."

I do not want you to be ignorant of this MYSTERY, brothers, so that you may not be conceited: ISRAEL HAS EXPERIENCED A HARDENING IN PART UNTIL THE FULL NUMBER OF THE GENTILES HAS COME IN. AND SO ALL ISRAEL WILL BE SAVED . . . (Rom. 11:25,26).

How will we know when we are at the fullness of the Gentile age? Jesus gets very specific when He talks about Jerusalem.

They [the Jewish people] *will fall by the sword and will be taken as prisoners to all the nations. JERUSALEM WILL BE TRAM-PLED ON BY THE GENTILES [BE IN NON-JEWISH POSSESION] UNTIL THE TIMES OF THE GENTILES ARE FULFILLED* (Luke 21:24).

On June 7, 1967, Israel possessed Jerusalem. This signified that the Gentile age was drawing to a close.

Other signs to expect at the fullness of the age are the salvation of Israel ("all Israel will be saved" Rom. 11:26) and an increase in anti-Semitism (the only way for satan to delay the return of Jesus).

Jews Who Believe in Jesus

Before 1967, when Jewish people accepted Jesus they usually joined the denomination of the person who led them to the Lord. For all practical purposes, they stopped being Jewish and their offspring then totally assimilated.

After 1967, a new phenomenon began to occur simultaneously all over the world. Jewish people who turned to Jesus began to say: "Something within me says that I am still Jewish and that I must preserve my Jewish identity." As this belief spread, Messianic Jewish Synagogues started springing up all over the world. Today, almost every city with a substantial Jewish population has one or more of these congregations.

Some have thought this movement might be a divisive factor among believers, creating a middle wall of partition in the Church. But Messianic congregations are made up of both Jews and

Gentiles that have become new creations. The primary differences that distinguish a Messianic Jewish congregation from a typical church are the presence of more Jewish believers and the biblical Jewish flavor of the worship. For instance, Jesus' death and resurrection are celebrated on Passover instead of on Easter. Also, there is an emphasis on Jewish evangelism.

Messianic Jews are a real enigma to the world. Traditional Jews and some Christians wish they would stop calling themselves Jews. But something in their hearts keeps saying, *"I was born a Jew and I will die a Jew."* Paul obviously felt the same way as he continued to identify himself as a Jew *after* receiving Jesus as his Messiah (Acts 21:39). From whom does this deep instinct come? God promised to preserve the Jewish people as a distinct group as long as there is an earth (Jer. 31:35, 36). Anyone who tries to prevent the Jewish people from surviving as a distinct people will find themselves fighting against God. This regathering of Jewish people to Jesus as Jews is no more of human origin than the reestablishment of modern-day Israel.

May 14, 1988 marked another milestone in this process. This day was the 40th anniversary of the rebirth of Israel. Messianic Jews had a dream of a Messianic Jewish gathering in Jerusalem on Shavuot (Pentecost) during Israel's 40th birthday. Over 1,400 registered for the conference — the largest gathering of Messianic Jews in Jerusalem in almost 2,000 years. All of Israel was talking about the Messianic Jews. Every major Israeli newspaper carried articles about them. And Israel became aware that Messianic Judaism was a credible, formidable movement.

Dahaf Research Institute of Tel Aviv, a respected, secular public opinion polling company, interviewed Israelis about

Messianic Jews and shocked the world with its results. Seventy-eight percent said a Messianic Jew had the right to be a citizen of Israel under the Law of Return.[24]

A Remnant Will Return

While there are many battles left for Israel to fight, the Jews that are stuck in the diaspora will suffer even worse judgment. God's Word says that only a remnant will survive:

Though I completely destroy all the nations among which I scatter you, I will not completely destroy you (Jer. 30:11).

A REMNANT will return, a REMNANT of Jacob will return to the Mighty God. Though your people, O Israel, be like the sand by the sea, only a REMNANT will return. DESTRUCTION HAS BEEN DECREED, OVERWHELMING AND RIGHTEOUS (Is. 10:21-22).

Our job is to tell every Jew (and Gentile) everywhere about Jesus before "destruction" comes.

Esther, we desperately need you to help your "younger brother," the prodigal son, who has come home. We haven't had the benefits of being raised and nourished in the Word as you have. We haven't had parents who have taken us to church. We haven't had grandparents praying daily that we would come to know Jesus. We have

24. "The Dahaf Report On Israeli Public Opinion Concerning Messianic Jewish Aliyah," p. 5. Interviews conducted January 17-24, 1988. Translated by Amikam Taver, with comments by David H. Stern, Ph.D. Copyright 1988 by David Stern, Jerusalem, Israel.

a lot of rough edges from our years of independence. But, Esther, we who have not come to know Jesus and we who have need your love, patience and prayers now more than ever.

CHAPTER EIGHT:

THE LARGEST ALIYAH

ESTHER, A MIRACLE IS HAPPENING RIGHT BE-FORE YOUR EYES AS THE SOVIET JEWS RETURN TO THE LAND OF ISRAEL. WHILE SATAN'S STRAT-EGY IS TO RID ISRAEL OF MESSIANIC JEWS, GOD IS FLOODING ISRAEL WITH SOVIET JEWISH BE-LIEVERS!

Removing the "Salt"

The same power that is fighting against Jews and Christians is especially at work against Messianic Jews in Israel. Although, according to the Dahaf Public Opinion survey, the majority of Israelis accept a Jew that believes in Jesus, there is a strong minority party that is trying to prevent Messianic Jews from making "aliyah" (immigrating to Israel). Why is this "religious party" trying to prevent aliyah? Why has the Supreme Court of Israel ruled that a Jew who believes in Jesus is not considered a

Jew for purposes of aliyah? What is the satanic logic behind this outburst of anger?

The devil is acting like Haman in the book of Esther. He wants to eliminate the Jews to stop Israel from being a Jewish nation. The easiest way for him to accomplish this task is by first removing the "salt" (Messianic Jews) from Israel so he can destroy it from within. Without the presence of a large body of Messianic Jews, he can move freely. Esther, it is only when you equip the Jew with the sword (the Word of God) that we can defend ourselves against the devil.

So far the devil has managed to destroy two million Jewish sabras (Israeli-born boys and girls) through abortion. More babies have been killed in their mothers' wombs since modern Israel has become a Jewish nation than the children Hitler massacred in the holocaust. At the forefront of the fight against abortion in Israel are Messianic Jews![25]

Lord Jakobovits, Chief Rabbi of the United Hebrew Congregations of the British Commonwealth, stated in the *Jerusalem Post* that the birth rate in Israel among Arabs is twice as high as Jews, "presaging a non-Jewish majority in the Jewish state within 10-15 years." With "sabras" leaving Israel for the golden calf of America at an alarming rate, the Arabs do not need an "intifada" to destroy Israel. They can wait the Jews out until they have such an overwhelming majority they can take over.

Worldwide there is a phenomenally low Jewish birthrate. The Harvard Center for Population Studies for the U.S. Bicentenary

25. Be'ad Chaim, Association for the Protection of the Unborn Child. P.O. Box 7974, Jerusalem, Israel.

forecasts that by 2076 American Jewry will be reduced to 10,420![26] While the overall Jewish population is shrinking, there is one exception. Lord Jakobovits says the number of Orthodox Jews are increasing through an unprecedented birthrate. He says that "the most intensely committed enclaves in Israel and the West, are now doubling their number every eight years. A spectacular increase probably without parallel in Jewish history . . . ." [27]

What is the devil's strategy in all of this? If the Orthodox become the majority in Israel, they will make it exceedingly difficult for Messianic Jews to live in the land.

The Russians Are Coming!

But God is rearranging the whole face of the world because Esther is praying and fasting. Suddenly, the walls of Communism are coming down. From a Christian perspective, the obvious benefit of this new freedom is that many people will now have the opportunity to hear the gospel. To the Jews in the Soviet Union, however, the greatest benefit is being permitted to emigrate. Israel is gearing up to receive more than one million Soviet Jews over the next few years. This will be the largest aliyah (immigration to Israel) in history. It should not be such a surprise because God told us about it many places in Scripture, such as Jeremiah 31:8: "See I will bring them from the land of the NORTH. . . . a great throng will return."

26. As cited in Maoz newsletter, June 1989, p. 1. Post Office Box 763100, Dallas, Texas 75276-3100.

27. As cited in Maoz newsletter, June 1989, p. 3.

The same phenomenon that occurred when the Jews returned to the newly created nation of Israel will take place when the Soviet Jews return. When the Arabs controlled the land it was as if the land had died. But when the Jews returned, the desert literally began to blossom. That is one reason it is now so appealing to the Arabs.

Initially, as Hosea prophesied, it will be a difficult adjustment for these new immigrants. Many will even have to live in tents as Hosea 12:9 says: ". . . I will make you live in tents again." But the same Jews (over 10% of whom hold Ph.D.'s) who could not save the economy of the Soviet Union will begin to prosper in Israel. With their help, Israel will lead the world in high technology, agriculture and science, and will enter a golden era. God's Word says in Psalm 102:16 that first He will rebuild Zion and then He will appear in His glory.

Perhaps this great prosperity will be what causes the Soviet Union to change its mind about letting the Jews go. According to Ezekiel 38 and 39, Russia will chase the Jews to Israel and meet the same end as the Egyptians of the Exodus.

A mystery of this passage is how the Soviet Union will be aligned with Iran and other Arab countries as well as European nations for the purpose of invading Israel. What does an atheistic country have in common with Moslem countries?

More than 25 percent of the Soviet Union is currently Islamic. A low ethnic Russian birthrate combined with a high Moslem birthrate is increasing this percentage. By the year 2000, Moslems will comprise over 50 percent of the Soviet army.

All these "strange bedfellows" have one thing in common. They want to see Jewish Israel wiped off the map![28]

Unprecedented Opportunity

Right now the Jews most open to the gospel in the United States are those who have immigrated from the Soviet Union. I have received reports of Jesus visiting Soviet Jews even while in the Soviet Union. Already, there are two Russian Messianic Jewish Synagogues in Israel. The congregation in Tiberias has 100 members.

Most of the Jews who are leaving the Soviet Union want to come to the United States. But the U.S. has limited the number who can come here, so the majority go to Israel. The leader of Israel's Labor Party, Shimon Peres, said, "I don't think there is anything more important in our own life than to have the Russian Jews come to Israel." I believe this statement is also true for God. This is the group He will use to usher in revival to Israel and to foil satan's strategy for the Orthodox to gain political control of Israel! Watch for the Soviet Union to use the Jews as bargaining chips with the Arabs. When they want something from the Arabs, Jewish emigration will slow down. *But God will foil their plans!* He will use miracles greater than during the exodus from Egypt to bring the Jews home.

28. From an interview with Ralph Mann on Messianic Vision radio broadcast #622 (broadcast September 1989).

CHAPTER NINE:

TIME IS RUNNING SHORT

ESTHER, HAVING JUST RETURNED FROM A FACT-FINDING TRIP TO THE SOVIET UNION, I AM CONVINCED MORE THAN EVER THAT TIME IS RUNNING OUT. YOUR HELP IS URGENTLY NEEDED!

"D-E-S-T-R-U-C-T-I-O-N!"

If you could enter a time machine and go back in history to June 1939, how passionately would you warn the German Jews to leave Germany? How much energy would you devote to rescuing these six million Jews that would shortly be exterminated?

After my recent fact-finding trip to the Soviet Union, I am convinced that another holocaust is in the making.

65

As I traveled through the streets of Odessa, a Soviet city in which half the people have Jewish blood, thoughts of the early radical Zionists like Ziev Jabotinsky came to mind. Jabotinsky was born in Odessa and witnessed his first pogrom (organized effort to kill, rape and rob Jews) in 1903.

As far back as 1932, Jabotinsky warned Jews to "do everything you can to get out of Europe, because the ground is burning under your feet!" In June 1939, he said:

"Zero hour is approaching. The hour of great destruction. D-E-S-T-R-U-C-T-I-O-N! Learn this word by heart! For three years I have implored you, appealing to you, warning you unceasingly, that the catastrophe is nigh. My hair has turned white, and I have grown old over these years, for my heart is bleeding that you do not see the volcano which will soon begin to spew forth its fires of destruction. I see a horrible vision. Time is growing short for you to be spared. I know you cannot see it, for you are troubled and confused by everyday concerns. For God's sake, let everyone save himself so long as there is time to do so, for time is running short!" [29]

While I was in Kiev, a Soviet Jew told me that his next-door neighbor was a Pamyat member. Pamyat is a high profile anti-Semitic organization. His neighbor said Pamyat requirements were for each member to kill a Jew. And with that, the neighbor looked him in the eye and said, "You are my Jew!"

29. As cited in "A Word from Jerusalem," in the January-February 1987 newsletter of the Internationl Christian Embassy, P.O. 1192, Jerusalem, Israel 91010.

Shockwaves rippled through the Jewish community from televised reports of a young, female Jewish attorney who was killed when her apartment was burned to the ground. This woman had been warned previously to leave Russia or be killed.

Another man shared how in 1977 anti-Semites broke into his house and murdered his son. The case was suspended because the authorities could not find the boy's body. In May 1988, this same man was beaten unconscious while at work. He was hospitalized with a fractured skull. Police agreed to investigate only after receiving two written complaints. However, when they found his name on the list of people waiting to leave the Soviet Union, they refused to speak with him.

A member of our tour group was entering the hotel elevator when a man grabbed the Jewish star around her neck and started yelling, "I hate you and I hate this!" As he attempted to drag her around a corner, she started screaming out the Lord's name. A couple heard her and came to her rescue.

The Horror Intensifies

Why this sudden increase in anti-Semitism? Why have over thirty anti-Semitic books been published in the Soviet Union in the past few years?

A Chasidic scholar told us he is certain the Soviet government endorses anti-Semitism. He pointed out that anti-Semitic groups can have meetings whenever they want. When he picketed one of their meetings, however, he was arrested. Also, one of Soviet leader Mikhail Gorbachev's key advisors is the leading anti-Semite, Valentin Rasputin, whom many consider to be the spiritual leader of Pamyat.

Many Soviet Jews believe things could get out of hand overnight. WHENEVER THE SOVIETS BEGIN TO LOOK FOR A SCAPEGOAT AND A RALLYING POINT, THE JEWISH COMMUNITY FEARS A POGROM IS IMMINENT.

Mind Games

When Hitler came to Kiev, he killed 33,000 Jews in the first five days. Jews know this history and many realize they must leave before it is too late. However, for most, it is a bureaucratic nightmare. The first requirement for emigration is to receive a written request from an Israeli citizen for that person to live in Israel. Many have to submit multiple requests before one gets through. Then, if they have a parent who does not want them to leave, they can't go. Many elderly parents feel they are too old to change countries. Even when all the paperwork is complete, it takes more than eight months to inventory the individual's possessions. And, because of transportation shortages, many have to wait up to a year to leave.

Many lose their jobs when they apply to leave. One woman told me the authorities play mind games with people. Forms are mysteriously lost, forcing applicants to fill out and submit another set. "Why don't you photocopy all the forms?" I asked.

She replied, "It's against the law."

68

The Gospel — A Ray of Hope

Against this deteriorating backdrop, a ray of hope is visible. Religious freedom has come to the Soviet Union. When our tour group took a train, we passed out tracts in Russian entitled, "Who is Jesus?" It was overwhelming to look down rows of passengers all hungrily reading about the gospel. I wish you could have seen the face of a woman in the hotel when I handed her a Bible. She acted as though I had given her $10,000. This was a far cry from the response of the average American Christian, who takes God's Word for granted. I have never in my life seen a people more hungry for the things of God.

There are more than sixteen million people in the Soviet Union who are at least one-quarter Jewish. Pamyat members plan to find those who are only even one-tenth Jewish and, as they put it, "finish what Hitler started."

I believe the door of religious freedom will be open for only a short while. We must bring the gospel to the Soviets before the iron curtain slams closed.

A Train Is Coming

A great miracle is about to take place in the Soviet Union. According to Jeremiah 16:14-15, it will so outshine the exodus from Egypt that people will no longer refer to this great miracle.

"However, the days are coming," declares the LORD, "when men will no longer say, 'As surely as the LORD lives, who brought the Israelites up out of Egypt,' but they will say, 'As surely as the LORD lives, who brought the Israelites up out of

the land of the north and out of all the countries where he had banished them. For I will restore them to the land I gave their forefathers.' "

If you draw a line on a map directly north from Jerusalem, it will intersect Moscow. God is saying that when you see the Soviet Jews coming home to Israel is the first step in a worldwide homecoming. When several million Jews were set free in Egypt, it was a great miracle. But how much greater will it be when the Jews around the world return home. Picture the Soviet Jews as an engine and the Jews scattered throughout the nations as the railroad cars. Once the engine takes off, the rest of the train is not far behind. One car is New York City, another is Buenos Aires, another is Paris. . . . The train is coming.

Handwriting on the Wall

Jeremiah goes on to say that fishers will come first to urge the Jews to return home. However, historically, the Jewish leadership has refused to see the handwriting on the wall until it was too late.

I interviewed Sam Stern, who was an orthodox rabbi in Poland before World War II. He was told by the Jewish leaders at that time that no harm would come to the Jews.

Although anti-Semitism is obviously on the rise, I met many Jewish leaders whose goal is to strengthen Jewish life in the Soviet Union. To them, certain religious freedoms are viewed as encouraging signs. For instance, while I was in Moscow, I attended a Passover Seder — the first public Passover Seder permitted in the Soviet Union in seventy years. My heart was heavy as I saw these

Jewish leaders falling for the same trap their forefathers did in Germany. According to Jeremiah 16:16, first the fishermen will come and then the HUNTERS, who "will hunt [the Jews] down on every mountain and hill from the crevices of the rocks."

When I told an American friend what I had observed, she was shocked. "How can the Soviet Jews not see the handwriting on the wall," she asked.

I responded, "How come you, as an American Jew, can not see the handwriting on the wall for America?"

Whom Are You Going to Believe?

The devil is desperately trying to circulate "bad reports" to discourage Jews from the U.S.S.R. and the rest of the world from making aliyah. He feels it will be easier to kill them in the diaspora than in Israel. The reports like those of the ten Jewish spies who explored Canaan are true. There are giants in the land. But there is a higher truth and a greater power — God's Word.

Drugs are rapidly getting out of control in Israel. The *Jerusalem Post* estimates Israel has 40,000 drug pushers.[30] As noted previously, the occult is growing supernaturally, and cults are rushing in to fill the spiritual vacuum.

American Jews assess the Israeli situation and respond as Esther first did; they are willing to send money but would not want to live there. This is understandable. Israel has one of the highest tax and inflation rates in the world. The bureaucracy makes even

30. As cited in an interview with David Wilkerson on Messianic Vision radio broadcast #637 (broadcast December 1989).

simple chores that we take for granted in the West to be major traumas. Military service is compulsory for all Israelis (except religious students), and many must give up one month per year for active service. And since Israel is surrounded by enemies that would like to drive them into the sea, military service is no country club. In short, the average American lives like a king compared to the average Israeli.

These are the bad reports we see in the natural, but never lose sight of the higher law. God's Word says, "We should go up and take possession of the land, for WE CAN CERTAINLY DO IT" (Num. 13:30). If you are a Messianic Jew, you must set your sights on aliyah. Where are the Joshuas and Calebs? Where are the true Jews, the Messianic Jewish pioneers? Israel needs you. God needs you. Enter the land before it is too late.

The shofar blast of God has gone out. The choice is whether to be a Joseph by heeding the times we are living in and preparing for the great Exodus to Israel by going ahead to the land, or being caught in Egypt.

"Come out of her, my people!"

Only the Orthodox and the Messianic Jews are obedient to the more than 700 Scriptures in which God promises the Land of Canaan to His chosen people and COMMANDS or encourages them to return to Israel. I can hear the echoes of Jeremiah's words blowing the shofar for aliyah.

Come out of her, my people! Run for your lives! Run from the fierce anger of the LORD.... You who have escaped the sword,

LEAVE AND DO NOT LINGER! Remember the Lord in a distant land and THINK ON JERUSALEM (Jer. 51:45, 50).

When the words of Zechariah and the other prophets begin to come to pass, there will be only one group of people that will stand with the Jews and Israel; it will be the true Church. Esther, you are in the valley of decision.

CHAPTER TEN:

STAND UP, ESTHER

The dividing line between true Christians and counterfeits has been drawn. Esther, if you do not stand up for the Jew in good times, you will not when it is life-threatening. Esther, Church, you failed God and the Jew at the time of Hitler's holocaust. You hid your Jewish connection just as biblical Esther refused to identify with the Jews at her first banquet with Haman and the king. But the second banquet (opportunity to spare the Jews) will soon be upon us. Esther, the words of Jabotinsky are still true: ". . . zero hour is approaching, the hour of great destruction. D-E-S-T-R-U-C-T-I-O-N!"

ESTHER, IT IS TIME TO STAND UP and make your voice known.

Do not think that because you are in the king's house you alone of all the Jews will escape. For if you remain silent at this time, relief and deliverance for the Jews will arise from another place,

75

but you and your father's family will perish. And who knows but that you have come to royal position for such a time as this? (Esth. 4:13-14).

PART II

"I BELIEVE IN JESUS

AS MY MESSIAH"

CHAPTER ELEVEN:

GRANDMA IS DEAD

ESTHER, I COME FROM A CLASSICAL JEWISH BACKGROUND. AS YOU WALK THROUGH MY EXPERIENCES, OBSERVING THROUGH MY EYES, YOU WILL HAVE AN UNDERSTANDING OF JEWISH PEOPLE THAT FEW NON-JEWS HAVE EVER GRASPED.

"Something Horrible Happened."

I had just returned from Israel and called home to ask my wife to pick me up from the airport. When my daughter Leigh answered the phone she was crying. I said, "What's wrong?"

"Something horrible happened," she said. "Grandma is dead."

Composing myself quickly, I tried to calm Leigh, by saying, "Grandma is in heaven."

"I know Dad, but I'm going to miss her."

After I hung up, it still did not seem real to me. My mother was such a memorable person it is hard for me to believe even today she is gone. When I needed money to pay for stolen coins I had purchased from mafia connections, she came through with no questions. My partner in crime could not believe I had a mother with such absolute blind faith and trust. When I went from job to job, she still loved and had faith in me. When I left my wife and daughter during an early mid-life crisis, she was hurt, but still loved and accepted me. When I walked out on a good career as an account executive with Merrill Lynch Stockbrokerage, she still loved me. When I got involved in an occult meditation course and started doing strange things with my mind, she still loved me. And when I told her I believed Jesus was the Jewish Messiah, she was unhappy, BUT SHE STILL LOVED ME.

"Do It Because I Said 'Do It'!"

Mom was born in Rochester, New York, and Dad in Poland. My father came from an Orthodox Jewish background, but Mom, although her grandfather was a prominent cantor in an Orthodox Synagogue, was Americanized in her Jewish expression.

Whenever I questioned many of our Jewish traditions, my father would respond by saying, "Do it because I said 'do it'! That's the way my father did it, and that's the way you have to do it." As I saw the hypocrisy connected with the expression of our faith, I rebelled. Since I was a child, I had no choice but to go to the synagogue with my parents. But I disliked every moment, sitting for hours hearing old men pray in a language I did not understand.

The best times were the Jewish holidays because we would have large family dinners and good food. At Passover we would leave an empty chair for Elijah. My father said one Passover he would visit us and announce the coming of Messiah. We would have a game of opening the door to see if Elijah were there. But like the Gentile child learns that there is no Santa Claus, I soon realized this was a fairy tale. We always ended the seder (Passover dinner) with a prayer, "Next year in Jerusalem." This also meant nothing to me.

There Must Be Something More

As a young man I had illusions of being a famous song writer. One of my songs was titled, "There Must Be Something More." The words went like this: "Because I work, eat, sleep and that's the way it goes ... There Must Be Something More." The desperation for more meaning in life was my heart's cry, even back then.

As a very young child, I remember one night being alone, when a strange thought crossed my mind. "What happens when you die?" In Judaism we never talked about death. Although we most definitely believed in life after death, we never discussed it. Judaism is a religion of Chayyim, life. So as I thought about death, since no one ever talked about it, my only logical conclusion was that I would cease to exist. Then I began to imagine what it would be like to no longer exist. The thought was so objectionable that I did the only thing possible, I blocked it from my mind.

As I grew older, if you had asked me if I believed in God, I would have said yes. But if you had asked me if I was a sinner, I would have said no. Compared to most of my Gentile (to me Gentile was synonymous with Christian) friends I was a pretty good person. Although I had an average Jewish education, bar-mitzvah, etc., I had not read the entire Bible and I was not sure it was true. I always had the feeling we Jews were better than the goyyim (non-Jews). And if you had asked if I was going to heaven, I would have said, "Sure." After all, I was Jewish. That is all that I thought was necessary. My father had drilled it into me that if we said a prayer for those that died, called the "Kaddish," somehow God would let them into heaven. And no matter what else I did, I could pray and fast on Yom Kippur and I would be forgiven. Although these would have been my answers, did I believe all this? Probably not. I was much more interested in Chayyim (life). And, since the tradition part of my religion seemed all that was necessary, I never gave any of these other issues much thought until many years later.

I Was Grateful, Very Grateful

It was the worst day of my life. My marriage was falling apart. My job was down the drain. And now I had opened myself up to the spirit world and I thought I was losing my mind. I was twenty-nine years of age and for the first time in my life I was told about Jesus. The only previous knowledge I had was not from what was said in my home, but from what was not said. I knew we Jews did not believe in Jesus, period. I remember being shocked when I read in Ripley's "Believe It Or Not" that Jesus was Jewish. You would think that a Jew who had lived twenty-nine years in "Christian" America would have known more about Jesus. I had not previously rejected Jesus. I knew nothing about Him.

Some Christian friends had shown me in the Torah that God condemned my involvement in the occult.

Let no one be found among you who sacrifices his son or daughter in the fire, who practices divination or sorcery, interprets omens, engages in witchcraft, or casts spells, or who is a medium or spiritist or who consults the dead. Anyone who does these things is detestable to the Lord . . . (Deut. 18:10-12).

I had been dabbling in many of these things for years. But now I had gone too far. I was in over my head. If you have ever read the book or seen the movie, *The Exorcist*, you can understand what I was experiencing. It was real. I needed help to escape but I did not know where to turn. Several days earlier my Christian friends had given me a booklet called "Four Spiritual Laws." Maybe I was in trouble with God. Maybe the Bible was real. I was so desperate, I was willing to try anything, even Jesus. I read the prayer to commit my life to Jesus and nothing happened. I figured it didn't work. Several days later, I gave up.

Remember my childhood fear of death? Well, life had become so horrible that death — ceasing to exist — looked better. That night I closed my eyes, not knowing or even caring if I would ever wake up. When I woke the next morning everything was different. The demonic spirit that had tormented me was gone. I had a peace inside of me that was as real as the fear that made me despair of life. And I knew Jesus was responsible for all this. I was grateful, very grateful. That was eighteen years ago. And I am still grateful.[31]

31. For a complete account of how Sid Roth became a believer in Jesus, read his autobiography, *Something for Nothing,* available for $5.00 through Messianic Vision, P.O. Box 34444, Bethesda, MD 20827.

CHAPTER TWELVE:

SOMETHING WRONG WITH THAT RABBI

ESTHER, WHEN PAUL SAID JEWISH PEOPLE HAVE SPIRITUAL SCALES OVER THEIR EYES, THIS IS WHAT HE MEANT.

My father was not even willing to let me talk about Messiah Jesus. After much prayer, however, he let me read to him the 53rd chapter of Isaiah. By the time I finished he was angry and accused me of reading from a Christian Bible[32] because I was reading

32. The major difference between a Jewish Bible and a Christian Bible is that the latter includes the New Testament. Also, the books of the Jewish Bible are in slightly different order and sometimes the verse number is different by one verse. For instance, Micah 5:2 is 5:1 in the Jewish Bible. The actual translation is essentially the same. One significant difference is in Isaiah 7:14 where the Jewish Bible says "young woman" instead of "virgin." However, as is pointed out in Chapter 18 of this book, this change is easily explained.

about Jesus. I showed him it was published by the Hebrew Publishing Company, but that was not good enough. He said he would only accept a Bible from his orthodox rabbi. "Hmm," I thought, "My father thinks Isaiah is speaking of Jesus."

So the next day I called our family rabbi for an appointment. When I entered his office, he greeted me with a warm welcome and asked what he could do for me. I asked if he would give me a Bible and inscribe something personal to me. He gladly gave me a Bible and wrote some kind words to me on the inside cover.

I thanked him and left quickly. I could not wait to show this powerful gift to my father. When I arrived, I confidently showed my Dad the inscription and made sure he read it. Then I began to read the same passage from Isaiah. Now he had only two choices. Either he had to agree Jesus was the Messiah or he had to think something was wrong with the rabbi. To my shock, he said, "I've always thought there was something wrong with that rabbi." And then he proceeded to tell me how he once saw the rabbi eating out in a restaurant on Yom Kippur — the day of fasting.

It is both sad and ironic to see the lengths to which my people will go not to believe in Jesus. I learned that it is important to plant the good seed of the Word, but only God could cause the increase.

CHAPTER THIRTEEN:

THINK FOR YOURSELF

ESTHER, THE SCRIPTURES OVERWHELMINGLY PROVE JESUS IS THE MESSIAH. BUT THE RABBINICAL FEAR OF JESUS IN RESPONSE TO CHRISTIAN ANTI-SEMITISM CARRIES MORE WEIGHT WITH JEWISH PEOPLE THAN YOU REALIZE.

My mother, a great peacemaker, convinced my father that my newfound belief in Jesus was a phase and that it too would pass. I was very concerned for my parents' salvation and tried to witness at every opportunity. My mother would listen, but my father would get angry and close his ears. Over the years my parents watched how my marriage was restored. They observed the new stability in my life. They could see I was becoming a real mensch (Hebrew word that, roughly translated, means "a good human"). They watched my wife, daughter, sister, brother-in-law and nephews become believers. When my sister lost her daughter by drowning in her back-yard swimming pool, my parents observed her inner strength in dealing with this tragedy — a strength that she had not had previously.

One afternoon when I went over to my parents' house for a visit, my father was at the race-track. I decided this was the time to prove to my mother that Jesus was the Messiah. I knew that she had very little knowledge of the Scriptures, did not know if they were true, and gave no thought to an after-life. The average Christian who saw my mother might have suspected differently. After all, she came from a religious family and attended an Orthodox Synagogue.

I started by trying to prove there is a God and the Bible is His book. "Mom, did you know the entire history of the Jewish people — past, present and future — is in the Bible? Hundreds of precise predictions have come true already. And the scientific dating of the Dead Sea Scrolls in Israel proves no one entered these predictions in the Bible after the event occurred.

"For instance, God said He would bless us beyond any people that have ever lived, if we would be obedient to His laws.[33] However, if we disobeyed we would lose our country, be persecuted and scattered to the four corners of the earth.[34] And wherever we would flee, we would be persecuted.[35] And, even though many of us would suffer and die, we would always be preserved as a distinct people.[36] With the suffering we have gone through as Jews, you would think every Jew left alive would have assimilated, as a

33. Deut. 28:1.

34. Deut. 28:36, 37; Is. 11:12.

35. Deut. 28:65.

36. Jer. 31:36.

means of self-preservation. But against impossible odds, God has preserved us as a distinct people.

"Then, in the last days a miracle would happen. Israel would become a Jewish nation.[37] If Israel were not a Jewish nation and the U.N. had to vote on it becoming a Jewish homeland today, what would the probability be? Zero would be too generous. That is how impossible it was in 1948. But God caused a great sign to occur that was of far greater magnitude than the crossing of the Red Sea as though it were dry land.[38] And a nation, Israel, was formed in a day, as Isaiah predicted.[39]

"Amos said once we returned we would REBUILD the waste cities.[40] And, if you investigate the history of Israel, you will find one city is built upon another. Tel Aviv is as modern and cosmopolitan as any city in the world. Isaiah even said the desert would blossom as the rose.[41] By the way, did you know Israel exports more ROSES to Europe than any other nation? Ezekiel prophesied the reforestation of Israel.[42] And Isaiah 35:7 tells us, 'The burning sand will become a pool, the thirsty ground bubbling springs.' How did Isaiah know 2,700 years ago that Israel would develop technology that would cause underground water to bubble to the surface and cause vegetation to grow in the barren desert? Since this water

37. Jer. 16:15

38. Jer. 16:14, 15.

39. Is. 66:8.

40. Amos 9:14.

41. Is. 35:1.

42. Ezek. 36:8.

comes from deep within the earth, it comes out warm, allowing growth in any weather![43]

"The only way Isaiah or any of the other prophets could know these things is if God told them. Two hundred years before Cyrus was born, Isaiah 45:13 identifies him by name and says God would use this Gentile to build the Jewish Temple and restore the cities in Israel. How did Isaiah know his name? And better still, how did God get a heathen to want to restore Jerusalem? Jeremiah prophesied that Israel would go into captivity in Babylon for exactly 70 years.[44] Guess how many years we were captive in Babylon? Mom, I could go on and on about the amazing predictions of the Bible that were written thousands of years before the fact, but would you like to know about our future? Since God has demonstrated 100 percent accuracy so far, it is reasonable to expect Him to know our future."

As I quickly moved from Scripture to Scripture, I could tell my mother was impressed with my knowledge of the Bible. And for the first time in her life she was confronted with the accuracy of the Scriptures.

"Mom, Zechariah says that in the last days the whole world will not know what to do with Jerusalem.[45] Today, the problems of Jerusalem and the tiny nation of Israel are in the news continuously. And Israel will be invaded by many nations. The

43. From an interview with Dr. Dov Pasternack of the Ben Gurion University of the Negev on "Report to Zion" radio broadcast #8 (broadcast April 1989).

44. Jer. 29:10 (70 years in Babylon).

45. Zech. 12:3.

invading powers are mentioned by name.[46] It will be a real blood bath; two-thirds of our people will perish.[47] And when there is no hope left, the Messiah will fight for Israel. Let me read it to you in Zechariah:

> *Then the Lord will go out and fight against those nations, as he fights in the day of battle . . . "They [the Jewish people] will look on me, the one they have pierced, and they will mourn for him as one mourns for an only child, and grieve bitterly for him as one grieves for a firstborn son. On that day the weeping in Jerusalem will be great . . ."* (14:3; 12:10, 11).

"Mom, do you know why we will be weeping?" I think this was the first time I paused for air and gave her a chance to speak.

"I guess because we will be so grateful for being spared," she said.

"That is partially right. But the main reason is because we will realize, for the first time, that Jesus is our Messiah, and we missed Him."

"But if Jesus is the Messiah why don't all the rabbis believe? Sidney, I love you, but you still don't know as much as the rabbis who have studied all their life," she said lovingly.

"Mom, the Talmud tells us that years ago, when the rabbis pondered how to recognize the Messiah, they concluded that there would be two Messiahs. One would suffer for the people and be

46. Ezek. 38:3-9.

47. Zech. 13:8.

like Joseph. He would be rejected by His own people. He is described in Isaiah 53:

He was despised and rejected by men, a man of sorrows, and familiar with suffering. Like one from whom men hide their faces he was despised, and we esteemed him not (v. 3).

"And, according to Daniel 9:26, He would die before the second Temple was destroyed:

After the sixty-two "sevens," the Anointed One [the Messiah] will be cut off and will have nothing. The people of the ruler who will come will destroy the city and the sanctuary.

"He would die by crucifixion. David describes this hundreds of years before the first recorded crucifixion. David even saw the guards gambling for His clothes. And he noted that His bones would not be broken because this is the requirement for acceptable sacrifices.

I am poured out like water, and all my bones are out of joint. My heart has turned to wax; it has melted away within me. My strength is dried up like a potsherd, and my tongue sticks to the roof of my mouth; you lay me in the dust of death. . . . They have pierced my hands and my feet. I can count ALL MY BONES; people stare and gloat over me. They divide my garments among them and cast LOTS FOR MY CLOTHING (Ps. 22:14-18).

"He did not die for His own sins but for OUR SINS.

. . . we considered him stricken by God, smitten by him, and afflicted. But he was pierced for our transgressions, he was crushed for our iniquities; the punishment that brought us peace was upon him, and by his wounds we are healed (Is. 53:4, 5).

"Incidently, the prophets go on to say His ancestry would be from the line of David,[48] the Gentiles would follow Him[49] and He would be born in Bethlehem of Judah.[50] Did you know His mother was living at the wrong place until shortly before His birth? Mary had to go to Bethlehem for a special census for tax purposes at the precise moment of His birth!"

"O.K. already, so why don't the rabbis see this?" she asked.

"Well, they saw this suffering servant Messiah and called Him 'Messiah ben (son of) Joseph.' But then they found just as many predictions about the Messiah reigning as King and ushering in an age of peace. They called Him 'Messiah ben David,' like King David. How did they reconcile these supposedly contradictory roles? Their theory was that there were two distinct Messiahs. But today it is clear that it is one Messiah with two appearances. First, he came to initiate the New Covenant prophesied by Jeremiah, to change us from the inside out.

"The time is coming," declares the Lord, "when I will make a new covenant with the house of Israel . . . and will remember their sins no more" (Jer. 31:31, 34).

48. 2 Sam. 7:12, 13.

49. Is. 11:10.

50. Mic. 5:2.

"Since we humans are so unclean compared to the holiness of God, we always needed a mediator and the blood of an innocent animal to atone for our sins. During Temple days our intermediary was a high priest. Today, our intermediary cleanses us from all sins, the Lamb of God who takes away the sins of the whole world. Then, when we are clean, He actually takes up residence inside our body, which becomes His temple.

"Speaking of two appearances of the Messiah, did you know the first time Moses identified himself as our deliverer we rejected him?[51] And the first time Joseph identified himself as our deliverer, his own brothers wanted to kill him.[52] Jesus fits this same pattern. His second appearance will be when He comes to rule the world and usher in an age of peace.

They will neither harm nor destroy on all my holy mountain, for the earth will be full of the knowledge of the Lord as the waters cover the sea (Is. 11:9).

"Today the rabbis teach us about His second coming, but never mention Messiah ben Joseph. I found out why when I participated in a debate with a rabbi at the University of Maryland. After the debate, I engaged a young orthodox rabbinical student in dialogue. I asked him to tell me who Isaiah was speaking of in the fifty-third chapter. He amazed me with his answer. He said, 'I can't tell you.'

" 'Why?,' I quickly asked. 'You know Hebrew better than I. Read it from your Tanakh (Old Covenant).' "

" 'No,' he responded, 'it would be a sin.' "

51. Ex. 2:11-14.

52. Gen. 37:8, 19.

" 'Why?,' I asked again."

" 'Because I am not holy enough,' he said. 'We can only tell you what the rabbis that lived closer to the days of Moses tell us the verse means.' "

"How sad, Mom. What he was really saying was he COULD NOT THINK FOR HIMSELF."

Although I thought my presentation to my mother was overwhelming, she let me know she was grateful for the change believing in Jesus had caused in my life, but was not ready to accept the truth. "What would your father say? Are you hungry? Can I get you something to eat?"

CHAPTER FOURTEEN:

"I BELIEVE"

ESTHER, YOU HAVE BEEN GIVEN A POWERFUL GIFT TO PIERCE STRONGHOLDS OF THE ENEMY OVER THE JEWISH PEOPLE. THIS GIFT COMES WITH A GUARANTEE FROM GOD. IT NEVER FAILS. IT'S CALLED LOVE.

One day I saw my mother walking up my driveway with what I affectionately called care packages. She loved to bring my sister and me groceries. As I watched, she fell down. I rushed out immediately to help her. My mother was a heavy woman and I could see she had done considerable damage to her knee. It was puffed up and began to turn all the colors of the rainbow. I was worried. I said, "Mom, can I pray for you?" When she lovingly agreed, I said under my breath, "Lord, if you ever answer a prayer, now is the time." And before my eyes and my mother's eyes, the swelling went down and the discoloration virtually disappeared.

After that healing, whenever my mother was sick, she would call me and expect God to heal her through my prayers. And she started adding a new phrase to her vocabulary. She would often express aloud the words "Praise the Lord."

Then one day my aunt, who had diabetes, developed gangrene of the big toe. Her Jewish doctor said the only way to save her foot was to amputate her toe right away. With that, my mother boldly asked the doctor, "Could we wait a day so my son could pray for her?"

"Lady," he replied, "not even Jesus Christ could save that toe."

Before God, the devil, the angels in heaven, my mother and the Jewish doctor, I proclaim to you my aunt's toe was never amputated.

And one day my mother said to me, "Sidney, I no longer believe in Jesus because of *your* faith. I believe in Jesus as my Messiah because *I* believe."

PART III

SHARING YESHUA

AT THIS POINT, ESTHER, YOU MIGHT BE WON-
DERING WHY MORE JEWISH PEOPLE DO NOT BE-
LIEVE IN JESUS, OR AT LEAST WHY THE RABBIS
DON'T. THE REASON IS THAT RABBINICAL JUDA-
ISM HAS DEVELOPED OBJECTIONS TO EVERY
BIBLICAL PROPHECY ABOUT JESUS. YOU HAVE
NEVER BEEN CHALLENGED BY A RABBI BECAUSE
RABBIS DO NOT CARE IF YOU AS A NON-JEW BE-
LIEVE IN JESUS. HOWEVER, AS MORE JEWISH
PEOPLE COME TO FAITH, THEY WILL NEED
YOUR HELP IN MEETING CHALLENGES TO THEIR
NEW-FOUND BELIEF IN JESUS. THIS PART OF THE
BOOK, PARTICULARLY THE "DIALOGUE" AND
"ADVANCED DIALOGUE" SECTIONS, WILL PRE-
PARE YOU FOR THIS TASK.

CHAPTER FIFTEEN:

WHO IS A TRUE JEW?

The Real Issue

As a young Jew growing up in a traditional Jewish home, I never focused on the question "Who is a Jew?" I was Jewish and that was that. Even though I was not really sure there was a God, I was still a Jew. Even though I only went to synagogue because I had to, I was still a Jew. Although I believed that the Torah was created by man, although I cared nothing about Israel, although I became involved in the occult, a practice emphatically condemned by Jewish law, I was still a Jew.

But when I rejected the occult, returned to my wife and daughter, became an ardent Zionist, and began attending Shabbat services because I wanted to please God and live according to His Word, many of my fellow Jews declared that I was no longer Jewish!

Actually, the real issue is not merely "Who is a Jew?" but "Who is a *true* Jew?" The word "Jew" comes from the Hebrew name "Yehudah" (Judah), which means "praiser of God." How could I have been considered a praiser of God as an Orthodox Jew when He was not relevant to my life? Certainly my behavior could not have been considered a "praise" to God.

Moses was a *true* Jew, a praiser of God. He had a reverential fear of the Almighty. He spoke to the Lord and the Lord answered. He prayed and miracles took place.

Today, as a Messianic Jew, I have this same relationship with God.

The Kaddish

After my mother's funeral, my father had only one question. Was I going to say the prayers (Kaddish) for my mother in the synagogue every day for eleven months? There was an ulterior motive behind my father's question. If I would say the prayers for my mother, he could be assured that I would say them for him. And it was his belief that somehow these prayers would be his ticket into heaven without punishment or delay. Since he knew I did not agree with this form of prayer, he wondered what my answer would be. For a split second I thought of the time commitment. I thought of the endurance needed to sit through all the rituals and prayers in a language I did not understand. I thought of the possible repercussions by those in the synagogue that knew of my outspoken faith in Jesus. But as quickly as these thoughts raced through my mind, I found myself agreeing to do it.

It had been years since I had put on the tefillin (little box with Scripture inside that is wrapped around one's head and arm to conform to Deut. 6:8). A retired rabbi helped me as I placed the tefillin around my arm and on my head. There was a good feeling in worshipping with my people and participating in rituals that have been observed for thousands of years.

After one service, I got into a conversation with the man who read from the Torah. The Torah reading happened to be about the Jewish people walking through the Red Sea as though it were dry land. As I discussed this with my friend, he looked at me with the most incredulous expression and said, "You don't really believe those stories, do you?"

I responded with just as incredulous an expression and said, "You don't? What are you doing here?"

It is one thing when a secular Jew does not believe in the Torah. But when a Jewish religious leader does not believe in the Torah, it shocks me. Then, when he told me he did not believe in God or life after death, I really was curious why he was even attending the synagogue. He responded, "Because my friends are here. Because I like the traditions of my fathers. And because it gives me something to do." I always thought these elderly men who davined (prayed) every day at the minyan (a gathering of ten or more Jewish men to pray) were the most tsaddik (holy) Jews in the synagogue. I found that many of these men I prayed with felt the same way as my friend.

My father greatly appreciated my going to the synagogue every day to pray. And since I had not mentioned Jesus in a while, he asked, "Do you still believe in Him?" I had been waiting for God's timing because every time I mentioned Jesus, my father would always get angry. I told him that I believed in Jesus and He was the reason I was going to the synagogue. I told him I did not believe the prayers were necessary for Mom because she was already in heaven. At that, he got angry and I quickly changed the subject.

On another occasion my father said men from the synagogue had told him that their sons would not have been so faithful to go to the synagogue every day. My father would say to me, "You're a wonderful son. You're as good as gold. But do you have to believe in *Him*?"

The Talmud declares that if a voice from heaven should contradict the majority of rabbis, we must ignore that voice. A *true* Jew says that if the Torah contradicts the majority of rabbis, we must follow the Torah.

May God grant that soon all Israel will be *true* Jews.

* * * * *

This is a unique time in history. God calls it the appointed time to have compassion on Israel (Ps. 103:13). You would not be reading this book unless God was raising you up to be a modern-day Esther. This is why God told me to write this book — to equip you to be able to answer the many sincere questions from Jewish people who are seeking Him. Esther, by the time you finish this section, you will be in a position for God to use you mightily for the salvation of Israel.

CHAPTER SIXTEEN:

THE BIBLE IS TRUE

These Scriptures will help you to establish the truth of God's Word. All prophecies are from the Jewish Scriptures.

Preservation of the Jewish People

This is what the LORD says, he who appoints the sun to shine by day, who decrees the moon and stars to shine by night, who stirs up the sea so that its waves roar — the LORD Almighty is his name: "Only if these decrees vanish from my sight," declares the LORD, "will the descendants of Israel ever cease to be a nation before me" (Jer. 31:35, 36).

Dispersion of the Jewish People

You who were as numerous as the stars in the sky will be left but few in number, because you did not obey the LORD your God.

. . . Then the LORD will scatter you among all nations, from one end of the earth to the other. There you will worship other gods — gods of wood and stone, which neither you nor your fathers have known (Deut. 28:62, 64).

Survival of the Jewish People

Yet in spite of this, when they are in the land of their enemies, I will not reject them or abhor them so as to destroy them completely, breaking my covenant with them. I am the LORD their God (Lev. 26:44).

Formation of Israel and Regathering of the Jewish People

In that day the LORD will reach out his hand a second time to reclaim the remnant that is left of his people. . . . He will raise a banner for the nations and gather the exiles of Israel; he will assemble the scattered people of Judah from the four quarters of the earth (Is. 11:11, 12).

Israel Rebuilt

They will rebuild the ruined cities and live in them . . . (Amos 9:14).

106

Agricultural Achievements

The desert and the parched land will be glad; the wilderness will rejoice and blossom (Is. 35:1).

Jerusalem: A Burden for All People

I am going to make Jerusalem a cup that sends all the surrounding peoples reeling. Judah will be besieged as well as Jerusalem. On that day, when all the nations of the earth are gathered against her, I will make Jerusalem an immovable rock for all the nations. All who try to move it will injure themselves (Zech. 12:2, 3).

All Nations Will Turn Against Israel

I will gather all the nations to Jerusalem to fight against it . . . (Zech. 14:2).

"In the whole land," declares the LORD, "two-thirds will be struck down and perish . . ." (Zech. 13:8).

CHAPTER SEVENTEEN:

SHALOM WITH GOD

Do the Jewish Scriptures talk about life after death? Daniel says:

Multitudes who sleep in the dust of the earth will awake: some to everlasting life, others to shame and everlasting contempt (Dan. 12:2).

How can we awake to everlasting life? By not being separated from God. The Bible says all of us are separated from God. We read in Psalm 14:3:

All have turned aside, they have together become corrupt; there is no one who does good, not even one.

And in Isaiah 59:2:

But your iniquities have separated you from your God. . . .

God gave us a way of "covering our sins" (atonement) through the sacrifice of an unblemished animal in the Temple:

It is the blood that makes atonement for one's life (Lev. 17:11).

Since the Temple was destroyed in A.D. 70, animal sacrifices for atonement are impossible. How can we have the blood of atonement today?

Jeremiah predicted a New Covenant for the house of Israel and Judah:

"The time is coming," declares the LORD, "when I will make a new covenant with the house of Israel. . . . and will remember their sins no more" (Jer. 31:31, 34).

God provided this New Covenant blood of atonement through a perfect sacrificial Lamb, one called "THE MESSIAH." Isaiah described how to recognize Him:

Who has believed our message and to whom has the arm of the LORD been revealed? . . . He had no beauty or majesty to attract us to him, nothing in his appearance that we should desire him. He was despised and rejected by men, a man of sorrows, and familiar with suffering. Like one from whom men hide their faces he was despised, and we esteemed him not. Surely he took up our infirmities and carried our sorrows, yet we considered him stricken by God, smitten by him, and afflicted. But he was pierced for our transgressions, he was crushed for our iniquities; the punishment that brought us peace was upon him, and by his wounds we are healed. We all, like sheep, have gone astray, each of us has turned to his own way; and the LORD has laid on him the iniquity of us all (Is. 53:1-6).

God made sure we could recognize the Messiah by giving us more than 300 identifying marks as described by the prophets of Israel.

HE WOULD BE BORN IN BETHLEHEM OF JUDAH.

But you, Bethlehem Ephrathah, though you are small among the clans of Judah, out of you will come for me one who will be ruler over Israel, whose origins are from of old, from ancient times (Mic. 5:2).

HIS ANCESTRY WAS TO BE FROM THE FAMILY OF DAVID.

"The days are coming," declares the LORD, "when I will raise up to David a righteous Branch.... This is the name by which he will be called: The LORD Our Righteousness" (Jer. 23:5, 6).

THE GENTILES WILL FOLLOW HIM.

In that day the Root of Jesse will stand as a banner for the peoples; the nations will rally to him, and his place of rest will be glorious (Is. 11:10).

HE WAS TO DIE *BEFORE* THE SECOND TEMPLE WAS DESTROYED.

After the sixty-two "sevens," the Anointed One will be cut off and will have nothing. The people of the ruler who will come will destroy the city [Jerusalem] and the sanctuary (Dan. 9:26). (In A.D. 70 the Temple was destroyed.)

Since God has provided the blood of Atonement through Messiah Yeshua (Jesus), we must repent (admit we have sinned and turn from unrighteousness) and ask for forgiveness in the name of Yeshua. Each individual's prayer should be: "Messiah Yeshua, I admit that I have sinned. I believe that You have provided the blood of Atonement for me. I receive You now as my Messiah. Thank You for giving me *shalom* with God."

CHAPTER EIGHTEEN:

DIALOGUE

"I was born a Jew and I will die a Jew!"

A Jewish person needs reassurance that he or she need not give up his Jewish identity to receive Jesus. On the contrary, he gains a personal relationship with the God of Abraham, Isaac and Jacob through his walk with the Jewish Messiah.

Nevertheless, years of misconceptions, mistrust and a lack of understanding of their own faith have contributed to certain arguments which Jewish people tend to raise when confronted with the Gospel.

To be effective, it is important that you be prepared to respond — in love — to these Jewish concerns:

"A person is either Jewish or Christian. I'm Jewish."

No, you are either Jewish, Gentile or of the Messiah. Non-Jewish (Gentile) followers of Messiah Jesus are called Christians; many Jewish believers in the Messiah prefer to be called Messianic Jews.

In our society, many who call themselves "Christians" are not true believers. Today's usage of the word "Christian" implies that a Jewish believer in Jesus is no longer Jewish.

"Doesn't belief in Jesus mean that you're no longer Jewish?"

This question really isn't the issue — it's a smokescreen! The question "How can you be Jewish and believe in Jesus?" is better answered with another question: "Who is Jesus?"

If Jesus, as claimed, is Israel's promised Messiah, then, according to the Scriptures, in order to be a truly observant Jew, one must acknowledge and believe in Jesus as the Messiah.

One is either Jewish or Gentile by birth — nothing can change that. According to the Bible, a Jew is a person who is descended from Abraham, Isaac and Jacob.

Jesus and His earliest followers were Jewish. They never renounced their Jewish heritage. Nor were they expected to do so. Believing in — and trusting — the Jewish Messiah can add to one's appreciation of Judaism.

"If Jesus is the Jewish Messiah, why don't more Jews believe in Him?"

Judaism today is divided into various groups: Reformed, Reconstructionist, Conservative, Orthodox and Hasidic. Each group accepts certain truths from the Talmud and certain truths from the Bible. The distinctive quality of Messianic Judaism is that it is biblically Jewish, i.e., it holds to the absolute authority of the Scriptures. This is important because to all other Jewish groups the *Bible is not the final authority.* Therefore, the Messiahship of Jesus in *not* an issue that is approached with an open mind, since the interpretations of today's rabbis depend totally on the opinions and traditions of their forefathers who rejected Jesus.

Those Jews who *have* studied the question of the Messianic claims of Jesus with a truly open mind have come to surprising conclusions, and many rabbis and Jewish leaders have indeed accepted Jesus as their Messiah. Some Jewish people have rejected Jesus because they fail to understand His dual role. They have looked for a king, a political leader who would free them from their oppressors and provide peace and prosperity. Jesus will accomplish this in the future, when He returns to re-establish the throne of David.

The Hebrew Scriptures indicate that the Jewish people would not recognize their Messiah when He first appeared (Is. 53:1-3) to die as an atonement for sin.

"We Jews believe in one God, not three."

Followers of Jesus also believe in one God, not three. Most Jews recite the Shema, the Jewish confession of faith, "Hear, O Israel, the LORD our God, *the Lord is one.*" However, the translation of the New Jewish Version, recognized as the most accurate English translation produced by Jewish scholars, states: "Hear O Israel, the LORD is our God, *the LORD alone.*" The point of the Shema is to demand absolute faith in the LORD alone, with no gods before Him. The Hebrew word *"echad,"* translated "alone" here, means "one" in the sense of "that one alone."

In the twelfth century, Moses Maimonides, writing to counter Christian and Muslim beliefs, compiled his thirteen articles of faith, recited by observant Jews daily. One of the articles states that Jews must believe that God is *yachid* — "absolute unity." But this is unscriptural, since the Hebrew Bible gives clear indications of God's composite unity

Genesis 19:24 states that "the LORD rained down burning sulfur on Sodom and Gomorrah — from the LORD out of the heavens." In other words, the LORD, *Who had been on the earth talking to Abraham* (read Gen. 18:1-33 very carefully), rained down fire and brimstone from the LORD *out of the heavens.*

The Spirit of God came upon many people in the Scriptures. For instance, Isaiah 61:1 states, "The Spirit of the Sovereign LORD is on me. . . ."

And, finally, Who is God's Son in Proverbs 30:4?

Who has gone up to heaven and come down? Who has gathered up the wind in the hollow of his hands? Who has wrapped up the waters in his cloak? Who has established all the ends of the earth? What is his name, and the name of his son? Tell me if you know!

Isaiah 42:1 speaks of God's servant (that is, the Messiah) upon whom God places His Spirit so that "he will bring justice to the nations." Here in one passage is a reference to the LORD (the Father), the Messiah (the Son), and the Spirit.

Here is my servant, whom I uphold, my chosen one in whom I delight; I will put my Spirit on him and he will bring justice to the nations.

"Jewish people don't need a middleman."

Judaism historically has required a priesthood, the Levites, to minister between the Israelites and their holy God. Leviticus 1:15 directed that only a priest (one of Aaron's sons) could sprinkle the blood of atonement in the Tent of Meeting for the forgiveness of sin.

Most Jewish people fail to understand that followers of Jesus now have direct access to God through the mediatorial role *performed* by Jesus. We now approach the LORD directly and go right into His holy presence. No Jew in Bible days, aside from the High Priest (and at that, only once a year) could ever do this.

"Jewish people do not believe in human sacrifice."

Followers of Jesus do not believe in this either. We as human beings have no right to sacrifice another human being for our sins. Only God has the absolute right to give life and take it away. Because the penalty for sin is death (Ezek. 18:4), God, in His great mercy, provided His own sacrifice to pay for the sins of the world. His own Son willingly suffered the death penalty for us.

It is the absolutely clear teaching of Isaiah 53 that God would place the punishment due His people upon an innocent and righteous sufferer Who would die for Israel's sins. This prophecy was fulfilled by Jesus the Messiah.

"Judaism does not believe in original sin."

Depending on one's definition of original sin, one may say that Judaism does or does not believe in this teaching. Psalm 51:5, which states, "Surely I was sinful at birth, sinful from the time my mother conceived me," clearly teaches the inherent sinfulness of man. And, according to some Jewish traditions, all human souls were in Adam when he sinned. Thus, when Adam sinned, the entire human race fell with him.

There can be no question, however, that the Hebrew Bible teaches the *universality* of sin. Genesis 8:21 says that "every inclination [Hebrew, *yetzer*] of [man's] heart is evil from childhood." And Ecclesiastes 7:20 says, "There is not a righteous man on earth who does what is right and never sins." Proverbs 20:9 asks, "Who can say, 'I have kept my heart pure; I am clean and without sin?'" And Isaiah 53:6 states that "We all, like sheep, have gone astray, each of us has turned to his own way." The sinfulness of man is a fact which is clearly taught throughout the entire Hebrew Bible.

"Religions are all alike. They all have some good points and can help people to lead worthwhile lives."

Faith in the Messiah is not a religion; it is God's declared way for mankind to be reconciled to Him. While there are many good points to commend in some religions, this does not mean that God is satisfied with everything in "religion."

What is important is *not* what man decides about God, but rather what God decides about man. We must approach God according to *His* standards. It is not up to us to devise our own way of approaching Him. Since He has given us a way to have our sins forgiven, then it is our *privilege* to accept His grace.

"Why did God allow six million Jews to die in the Holocaust?"

The secret things belong to the LORD our God, but the things revealed belong to us... (Deut. 29:29).

God has chosen to keep some of the reasons for the holocaust a mystery. But some reasons have been revealed.

God tells us that if the Jewish people were obedient to the law, they would be a nation of priests and blessed above all people on the face of the earth. However, if they violated the law, they would lose their homeland and be scattered to the four corners of the earth. And wherever they would go, they would be persecuted (Deut. 28).

119

It was as if God's law were a picket fence of protection around His people. However, once they went out of the gate of protection, they would be destroyed!

In addition to this warning in His Word, God always sent prophets who called for repentance with the hope that judgment could be averted. Sometimes the people repented, as in Nineveh when warned by Jonah, and sometimes they ignored God's message, as in Jerusalem when Jeremiah warned of Nebuchadnezzar's invasion. Before the holocaust of Hitler, God warned His people through fiery Zionists like Theodor Herzl and Ze'ev Jabotinsky. In 1939, Jabotinsky said, "I see a horrible vision. Time is growing short for you to be spared."

Even with the warnings, why a God of love allowed the holocaust is a secret that we will not fully understand until we get to heaven.

"What happens to Jews who do not believe in Jesus?"

The only way to be granted forgiveness of sin is belief in Jesus. Jesus said, "Hear, O Israel, the Lord our God, the Lord is one" (Mark 12:29). This is called the *Shema* and is chanted by God-fearing Jews.

Jeremiah (29:13) says, "You will seek me and find me when you seek me with all you heart."

Some believe that many Jews, sincerely seeking God, died with the Shema on their lips and had revelations of Jesus in concentration camps and during other times of trial and tribulation.

Only God knows those who are seeking Him with all their heart. We cannot know what is in any heart but our own. Who do *you say Jesus is?*

"How can a virgin have a child?"

Is anything impossible for God? Sarah gave birth to Isaac when she was past ninety. Besides, which is more difficult: for a virgin to conceive, or for God to create a human being from dust?

Actually, Messianic prophecy indicates that while Messiah was to be a real man, He was also to be greater than any man, one of His titles even being "Mighty God" (Is. 9:6; 9:5 in some versions). The virgin birth explains how this could be possible: Messiah would be born by human and divine means.

The Hebrew word in Isaiah 7:14 can *today* be translated "virgin" or "a young unmarried woman." Interestingly enough, when Jewish scholars translated Isaiah 7:14 into Greek (Septuagint) about two hundred years before Jesus, they translated the Hebrew word 'almah with the Greek word parthenos which means "virgin." And it is this Jewish translation which Matthew quoted in Matthew 1:23.

It is clear that the Messiah, Who was to be a special and supernatural person, had a special and supernatural birth.

"Christians have always hated and persecuted the Jewish people."

Not everyone who calls himself a Christian is a Christian. Jesus, Who commanded His followers to love all men, said:

Watch out for false prophets. They come to you in sheep's clothing, but inwardly they are ferocious wolves. By their fruit you will recognize them (Matt. 7:15-16).

If a person does not bear the Christian "fruit" of love, compassion and mercy, then he has no right to call himself a Christian.

"Do Jews need to repent?"

The Hebrew word for "repent" is *shuv* (pronounced SHOOV), and it literally means, "turn, turn back." Many times God spoke through His prophets to Israel saying: "Turn back to Me and I will turn back to you" (see, e.g., Zech. 1:3-4; Joel 2:12-14). In other words, if Israel would *repent*, then God would *relent*.

But do Jews need to "turn back" today? The answer is emphatically "Yes!" since: 1) all Jews are members of the human race; 2) all human beings sin; 3) whoever sins "turns away" from God; and 4) whoever has "turned away" needs to "turn back"!

Have you sinned in thought, word, or deed? Have you stolen something, or committed a lustful act, or hated someone in your heart, or been ungrateful, or abused your body, or told a lie, or been filled with pride? Is there any way at all, be it large or small, that you have turned away from God? Then whoever you are, Jew or Gentile, you need to repent ("turn back")!

"Doesn't Isaiah 53 refer to the Jewish people as a whole?"

The earliest Jewish interpretations of this chapter, which really begins with Isaiah 52:13, referred it to the Messiah. It is clear for many reasons that it *cannot* refer to the Jewish people as a whole, or even to a righteous remnant within the nation. This passage also *cannot* refer to the "Messianic Age" because verse three would then have the people reject a utopia: "He was despised and rejected by men, a man of sorrows . . . " (Is. 53:3). Furthermore, Israel has never been a silent sufferer: ". . . so he did not open his mouth" (Is. 53:7b). And who is "my people" if "He" refers to Israel? ". . . For he was cut off from the land of the living; for the transgression of my people he was stricken" (Is. 53:8b).

The prophet Hosea describes Israel as a harlot. Israel, unlike the Messiah described in the passage, is *not* without sin: ". . . nor was any deceit in his mouth" (Is. 53:9b).

Furthermore, according to the Torah, the Jewish people would only suffer if they were *un*righteous. Nowhere is it ever taught that Israel would suffer for the sins of the world. Only Jesus has ever fulfilled this prophecy.

CHAPTER NINETEEN:

ADVANCED DIALOGUE

by Dr. Michael Brown

The New Covenant

"The New Covenant is anti-Semitic. It is filled with negative references to the Jewish people, and it blames them for the death of Yeshua."

It is not difficult to show that the New Covenant is definitely *not* anti-Semitic. First, consider these facts:

1) All of the authors of the New Covenant, save one, were Jews. Their main topic was Yeshua, the Jewish Messiah, and much of their writing was addressed to a Jewish audience (e.g., the Gospel of Matthew or the Letter to the Hebrews).

2) The New Covenant has many positive things to say about the Jewish people. Yeshua himself taught that "salvation is from the Jews" (John 4:22b), and Paul (Saul) said that the Jewish people were "loved [by God] on account of the patriarchs" (i.e., Abraham, Isaac and Jacob; Rom. 11:28b). In fact, Paul claimed that, from a spiritual standpoint, there was much advantage "in every way" in being born Jewish (Rom. 3:1-2), and that the Gentiles owed the Jewish people a material blessing, since they had partaken of the Jews' spiritual blessing (Rom. 15:27).

3) The heavenly city of Jerusalem, which is *the final destiny of all believers in Yeshua,* is said to have "a great, high wall with twelve gates" and the names written on these gates are "the names of the *twelve tribes of Israel*" (Rev. 21:12). In other words, *the only way into heaven is through Israel's gates.* This hardly sounds anti-Semitic!

What about the claim that the New Covenant also has many *negative* things to say about the Jewish people? Again, several answers can be given. First, the Hebrew prophets called their own people rebels, stiff-necked and sinful, and they predicted that judgment would come upon them if they did not repent. This is exactly what God told His Jewish people. Were the Hebrew prophets anti-Semitic? Or is God anti-Semitic? Of course not! But these are the very things that the Jewish writers of the New Covenant said about *their own people* — that because they rejected the Messiah they were being just like their forefathers, stiff-necked and sinful, and that for this they would be judged. Does this make the New Covenant anti-Semitic?

Also, it is important to note that the term "Jews" in the New Covenant often refers to "Judaeans," or even "Judaean religious leaders." Thus, some of the negative comments spoken in the Gospel of John against "the Jews" are not meant to apply to *all* Jewish people, but rather to specific Jewish leaders in Judaea. For a clear example see John 9:22, where the *Jewish parents* of a blind man who had been miraculously healed were afraid of *"the Jews"* (i.e., some Pharisees; see 9:13-15, 40-41). Similarly, the Hebrew word *yehudi* (pronounced ye-hoo-DEE) can either mean "Jew" or "Judaean." This explains a verse *in the Hebrew Scriptures* like Nehemiah 2:16, where Nehemiah, himself a Jew, refers to *another group* called "the Jews" (i.e., the inhabitants of Judaea), along with the priests, nobles, officials, "or any others who would be doing the work," all of whom were Jewish as well!

Finally, while some have claimed that Paul told his Gentile readers (in this case the Thessalonians) that *the Jews* "displease God and are hostile to all men," it is important to read the overall context carefully (1 Thess. 2:14-16). When this is done, it will be seen at once that Paul is speaking about *those* Jews "who killed the Lord Jesus and the prophets," and now persecute us "in their effort to keep us from speaking to the Gentiles so that they may be saved." And this, says Paul, is exactly what the Thessalonians were suffering from *their* own countrymen (i.e., not *all* Thessalonians, but rather those who opposed the faith).

When all these facts are considered with an open mind, it is quite clear that the New Covenant is *not* an anti-Semitic work. Thus many scholars today emphasize that if you want to understand the New Covenant fully, you must read it as a thoroughly Jewish Book!

"The New Covenant is full of historical inaccuracies. It frequently misquotes and misunderstands the Hebrew Scriptures."

As far as the historical accuracy of the New Covenant is concerned, it should be noted that of *every* book written in the ancient world, the Greek New Covenant is far and away the best preserved. There are literally *thousands* of ancient manuscripts containing copies of either part or all of the New Covenant books. And, in spite of the abundance of ancient manuscript evidence, these documents contain virtually *no disagreements* on any major doctrinal point.

As more and more research has been done into the customs and history of first-century Palestine and Asia Minor, the New Covenant has emerged as a prime historical source of great value, either confirming or supplementing what archaeology has taught us. Furthermore, studies by modern Jewish scholars have served to underscore the Jewishness of Jesus and the New Covenant authors.

The New Covenant's use of the Old Covenant has also been found to be thoroughly Jewish. Because the New Covenant was written in Greek while the Old Covenant was written in Hebrew, the writers often quoted from the Greek version of their day, the Septuagint. But this version was made by *Jews* some two hundred years *before* Yeshua was born. And although on certain occasions the *wording* of an Old Covenant verse may seem to change when it is quoted in the New Covenant, this is often due to the fact that the *Jewish Septuagint* was being quoted! These "differences," then, do *not* reflect later, "Christian" changes; and, more importantly, the *actual meaning* of the verses *never* changes.

Another major factor to be considered is that the New Covenant writers, who, with the exception of one medical doctor, Luke, were all Jews, often followed the *Jewish interpretative rules* of the day. It was as Jews that they read their Scriptures, and it was as Jews that they interpreted their Scriptures! Thus, some of their quotations of the Hebrew Scriptures are in keeping with the *common Jewish understanding* of the passage which they were citing. At other times, the main difference in interpretation was due to the fact that they understood that the Messiah had *already come*, and, rather than waiting for a future fulfillment of the Scriptures, they saw them as already being fulfilled. And there are some New Covenant quotations which reflect the interpretation found in the Aramaic paraphrases (called Targums — "translations") which were then being read in the *synagogues*. Again, this means that the New Covenant writers were being thoroughly *Jewish* in their handling of the Hebrew text.

It is also important to remember that the Jews in the first century of this era were primarily concerned with determining what the Scriptures were saying to *them*, in their day and age. Their primary concern was not in rediscovering what Amos or Isaiah had said to *his* contemporaries. They wanted to know what God required of them in the present tense, and they wanted to know what He had promised them. Thus, the Jews who authored what we now call the Dead Sea Scrolls moved into an isolated life of study and discipline *based on their interpretation of the Hebrew Bible*. The Pharisees began to develop a detailed system of laws and regulations *based on their interpretation of the Hebrew Bible*. And the writers of the New Covenant received and followed Yeshua as Messiah *based on their interpretation of the Hebrew Bible*.

Of these three different systems of Jewish interpretation, that of the New Covenant most accurately adheres to the proper understanding of the Hebrew text. In fact, in comparison to the *Jewish* interpretation of Scripture as found in the Talmud and Midrash, the New Covenant writers were amazingly careful and sober.

Any time the New Covenant interpretation does seem hard to follow, one need only remember these three facts: (1) the writers may have been quoting the Septuagint, the *Jewish* Greek version of the day (the *wording* may be slightly different, but the meaning is the same); (2) they may have been following an unusual *Rabbinic* method of interpretation (while our twentieth-century Western minds may have a hard time following their line of reason, a first-century rabbi would have had no problem grasping their point); and (3) they were able to find hints and indicators of Messiah's life and ministry on virtually every page of the Hebrew Bible, since, along with many other first-century Jews, they rightly believed that all the Hebrew prophets and the entire history of ancient Israel pointed to the coming of the Messiah. Therefore, although they did not disregard the original contextual meaning of the passages which they quoted, their primary purpose was to show how wonderfully all Old Covenant history and revelation were brought to their fullness (i.e., were fulfilled) in Yeshua the Messiah.

Although many Jews of today claim that the New Covenant authors contradict themselves, not a single Jew in ancient times ever raised such an argument! If there were so many gross errors and mistakes, why didn't those who opposed the faith point these things out back then? The answer, of course, is that according to all standards of ancient history writing, the New Covenant documents were a first-rate piece of work. And if, as some claim, the

Jews who wrote the New Covenant were cunning men who were willing to lie and deceive, then why didn't they make up a story that no one could argue with, not even their opponents? Obviously, they were just reporting the facts as they saw them, and none of their contemporaries could disagree!

One early follower of Yeshua pointed out that there is an amazing *overall harmony* which exists in the Gospel accounts of our Messiah. He stated that any *apparent* discrepancies which might be noticed could be explained only if we understood that each of the eyewitnesses was accurately reporting what he saw and heard. Thus, if we ourselves were there at the time the event occurred, we would see how perfectly all the pieces of the puzzle fit together to form one clear picture of the life and teaching of the Son of God. Therefore, rather than being evidence of poor memory and lies, the different perspectives of the various New Covenant authors help us realize just how accurate their accounts really were.

Some of the greatest minds this world has ever seen have devoted their entire lives to the careful study of the New Testament text, and some of history's greatest skeptics have attacked it. *There is nothing new that today's critics will discover.* The New Covenant has endured the test of time. It continues to be worthy of our faith.

"Yeshua didn't fulfill any of the Messianic prophecies. We know that the New Covenant writers actually reconstructed the life of Yeshua so as to harmonize it with certain predictions made by the prophets."

These two statements are mutually contradictory. Why would the New Covenant writers *intentionally* rewrite the events of Yeshua's life so as to make Him fulfill predictions that were not really Messianic? If the prophecies which they quoted were really non-Messianic, then why did they "make" Yeshua's life conform to them?

We can be confident that the Gospel writers accurately depict the events of Yeshua's life, since it is recorded that even they were baffled by His suffering and death. They had different ideas of what the Messiah would do when He came, and so they could not understand much of what occurred as the *fulfillment* of Old Covenant prophecy. It was only *after* Yeshua's resurrection that these men were able to see how all the events of His life and death were spoken of by the prophets of old.

Now, the point of all this is simple: If the disciples were going to *rewrite* Yeshua's life story as a witness to their own people, why didn't they make it line up with some of the more "orthodox" Jewish expectations? Why did they make it run contrary to much of the popular feeling of the day? And why did they write a story that would surely go against the grain? Simple! It was just as Peter told the Jewish authorities who challenged him: *"For we cannot help speaking about what we have seen and heard"* (Acts 4:20). They were true eye-witnesses; they saw it all. They could only give it to us the way it happened to them.

As to the statement that, according to the New Covenant account of the life of Yeshua, He did not really fulfill any truly Messianic prophecies, one might well ask, "Messianic prophecies according to whom?" According to one statement in the Talmud (Sanhedrin 99a), *all* the prophets prophesied of the days of the Messiah, a statement echoed by Peter in Acts 3:22-24. Who says that Isaiah 2:1-4, speaking of the days of universal peace, is Messianic, while Isaiah 53, speaking of one man dying for the sins of the nation, is *not* Messianic? Who says that Numbers 24:17, speaking of the destruction of Israel's enemies, *is* Messianic, while Daniel 9:24-27, speaking of the death of the Anointed One (Hebrew *mashiach*), is not Messianic?

The only reason why certain prophecies of a suffering Savior have been considered non-Messianic by certain strands of Judaism is due to the fact that if they were acknowledged as being Messianic then Yeshua would have to be the Messiah! Since He was, in fact, rejected by many Jewish rabbis, the next step was to reject as Messianic the prophecies that foretold His suffering and death.

"If the death of Yeshua really inaugurated the New Covenant spoken of by Jeremiah the prophet, then why hasn't it been fulfilled?"

Any covenant God makes with man has *conditions* and *goals*. First, there must be people who are willing to accept the stipulations of the covenant. Exodus 24:3 records that "when Moses went and told the people all the LORD's words and laws, they responded with one voice, 'Everything the LORD has said we will do.' " If some Israelites refused to accept God's covenant, then they would be cut off, but the covenant would still be binding and valid for those who did hear and obey.

For those people who did have a heart to follow God, the goals of the covenant would then be set forth. Exodus 19:5-6 records the *ideal goals* of the Mosaic Covenant: "Now if you obey me fully and keep my covenant, then out of all nations you will be my treasured possession. Although the whole earth is mine, you will be for me a kingdom of priests and a holy nation." Yet, even though this promise has never been fulfilled in the history of our nation, no one would dare question the validity and the authority of the Torah, because it is we who have failed to keep our part of the bargain.

Those who have accepted the New Covenant stipulations, ratified with Yeshua's own blood (Matt. 26:28), can bear witness that the promises and goals of the New Covenant are being fulfilled in them. God's law is now written in their minds and in their hearts, and the LORD has forgiven their iniquity, and remembers their sins no more (see Jer. 31:33-34, verses 32-33 in some versions). One day, when all Israel turns to Messiah Yeshua, the New Covenant will reach its fulfillment in the people as a whole. Until then, the *goals* of the New Covenant are being fulfilled in those who willingly accept its *conditions.*

The Messiah

"Judaism doesn't believe in a divine Messiah."

Judaism does believe in an *exalted* Messiah, higher than Abraham, higher than Moses, and higher than David (see, for example, the Midrash to Is. 53:12). And, according to Psalm 110:1, the LORD would say to Messiah (David's LORD), "Sit at my right hand until I make your enemies a footstool for your feet." Also, based on Jeremiah 23:6, some early rabbis offered the opinion that one of Messiah's names would be Yahweh. And Judaism does teach the *preexistence* of the Messiah, as one created before the worlds began.

More importantly, the Hebrew Scriptures clearly teach the divine nature of the Messiah. According to Isaiah 9:6 (9:5 in some versions), the King whose government and rule would have no end would be called *"Wonderful Counselor, Mighty God, Everlasting Father, Prince of Peace."* Although some Jewish interpreters tried to refer this passage to Hezekiah, king of Judah from about 715-687 B.C.E., he clearly was not the one described by Isaiah. His kingdom most definitely did come to an end, and, as a mere man, he could hardly be called *'el gibbor*, "Mighty God." In fact, "Mighty God" is used as a title of the LORD Himself in Isaiah 10:21! Modern Jewish translations of Isaiah 9:6 (9:5) that seek to soften the clear statement of Messiah's deity must ignore the most obvious meaning of the original Hebrew text.

"Judaism doesn't believe in a suffering Messiah."

Although this statement is commonly made, there is almost no truth to it. The Talmud records the teaching of more than one rabbi to the effect that Messiah son of Joseph (Hebrew — *mashiach ben yoseph*) would suffer and die in the great war that would precede the reign of Messiah son of David (Hebrew — *mashiach ben david*). In fact, Zechariah 12:10, which says, "They will look on me, the one they have pierced," quoted with reference to the death of Yeshua in the New Covenant, is applied to Messiah ben Joseph in the Rabbinic writings! It is also noteworthy that Isaiah 52:13-53:12, the clearest prophecy of a suffering Savior found in the Old Covenant Scriptures, is applied by the Targum to the Messiah, and Jewish exegesis up until approximately A.D. 550 interpreted this section almost exclusively with reference to the Messiah. Since then, the idea of a suffering Messiah has been present in many forms of Judaism, and descriptions of the Messiah's sufferings are especially rich in medieval mystical Jewish literature.

135

"Judaism doesn't believe that the Messiah will come twice."

Again, this statement is a smokescreen. First, as noted above, the Talmud mentions *two* Messiahs, one who will suffer and die, and one who will rule and reign. Yet the Hebrew Scriptures know only one Messiah, descended from David. Therefore, rather than creating a *second* Messiah descended from a *different* tribe, the New Covenant writers correctly saw that there would be only one Messiah Who would come *twice*. His first coming would be to fulfill the prophecies of a righteous sufferer Who would pay for the sins of the world. His second coming would be to establish His reign of peace on the earth.

One other point of special notice is that statements such as *"Judaism doesn't believe . . ."* are often totally misleading, seeing that from one Jewish group to another there may be totally different beliefs on such important subjects as the Messiah, life after death, oral law, and even God Himself! Thus, one can find within Judaism the opinion that Messiah was created before the world began, and He has been waiting in every generation to be revealed; or, that Messiah has *already been on earth* in every generation, waiting to be revealed; or, Messiah will come when the world is totally righteous; or, Messiah will come when the world is totally wicked; or, Messiah is more than a mere man; or, Messiah is only a mere man; or, Messiah is a concept; or, Messiah is a myth. Therefore, to say, "Judaism doesn't believe in a suffering Messiah, or in a Messiah who comes twice," is to give the false impression that Judaism has one set of beliefs regarding the person and work of the Messiah, and that these beliefs absolutely exclude the notion of a suffering Messiah or of a Messiah who would come twice.

"The Messiah is David's son. If Yeshua were really born of a virgin, then Joseph was not His father and He is really not a descendant of David. Therefore, Yeshua cannot be the Messiah."

According to Yeshua's own words, the Messiah was at one and the same time David's *son* and David's Lord (see Matt. 22:41-46), and the New Covenant is careful to show how the natural son of David could also be the spiritual Son of God. Thus, Matthew's genealogy provides the *royal* and *legal* descent of Yeshua carried through His adoptive father, Joseph, while Luke's genealogy provides His *natural* and *physical* descent through Miriam, His mother. In this way, the virgin-born Son of God, greater than David, has become the royal Messiah, descended from David. Therefore, rather than the virgin birth presenting a problem for the Messiahship of Yeshua, it actually provides a proof.

"Yeshua cannot be the Messiah, because He is a descendant of King Jehoiachin. God cursed both this king and his offspring, saying that none of his descendants would ever sit on the throne of David."

This argument can be answered in two very simple ways. First, it must be noted that Yeshua is *not* a natural, physical descendant of Jehoiachin (also called Jeconiah or Coniah), but only a legal descendant. Thus, only Matthew traces Yeshua's lineage through this king, while Luke's genealogy follows a different line. (Note carefully: the Shealtiel and Zerubbabel of Matthew 1:12 are probably *not* the same as the Shealtiel and Zerubbabel of Luke 3:27. This can be seen by noting that the name of Shealtiel's father in Matthew 1:12 is none other than Jeconiah, while in Luke 3:27 Shealtiel's father is Neri. Thus, Luke's genealogy of Yeshua does

137

not include Jeconiah.) Therefore, even if all of Jehoiachin's physical descendants *were* cursed, Yeshua would not have actually been under that curse.

More important, however, is that the Hebrew Scriptures plainly show that God did not curse all of Jehoiachin's descendants, but only his immediate offspring. In other words, God was not declaring that, for all time, none of Jehoiachin's descendants would ever sit on David's throne, but rather that his sons *who were then alive* would not rule. According to Jeremiah 22:24, God said: "even if you, Jehoiachin . . . were a signet ring on my right hand, I would pull you off." And then in verse 30 He commanded: "Record this man as if childless, a man who will not prosper in his lifetime, for none of his offspring will prosper, none will sit on the throne of David or rule anymore in Judah."

Apparently, there were Jews living in Babylonian exile who hoped that their people would soon break the yoke of the Babylonians, allowing either Coniah (i.e., Jehoiachin) or one of his sons to reassume the rule in Jerusalem. Jeremiah categorically stated that this could not be, for seventy years of captivity were determined for the Jewish nation, and neither Jehoiachin nor his sons would rule again. But, two generations later, Zerubbabel, *Jehoiachin's grandson,* became governor of Judah, *and the Messianic promises were renewed through him.* Thus, the prophecy that God would shake heaven and earth and overthrow the Gentile kingdoms was spoken to Zerubbabel (Hag. 2:21-22), and in the very next verse the LORD declared: " *'I will take you, my servant Zerubbabel . . . and I will make you like my signet ring* [that's right, a signet ring! Coniah, even if he were a signet ring on God's hand, was rejected. Zerubbabel would actually *be* a signet ring to the

138

LORD], *for I have chosen you,*' declares the LORD Almighty." In addition to all this, Zerubbabel became so famous in later Jewish literature that he is even mentioned in a Hanukkah prayer ("Well nigh had I perished, when Babylon's end drew near; through Zerubbabel I was saved after seventy years")!

It is impossible that Zerubbabel, Coniah's grandson, was under the curse, since he did in fact prosper (the curse said, "*none* of his [i.e., Coniah's] offspring will prosper"); and, as a son of David, he did govern the Jewish people. It is altogether fitting, then, that Matthew traces the royal line of Yeshua through Jeconiah (i.e., Jehoiachin), since the promises to David were renewed and confirmed in Zerubbabel, his grandson.

The Atonement

"The notion that we Jews need a blood atonement is completely wrong. First, even the book of Leviticus indicates that at certain times flour was accepted for an atonement, while Exodus 30 refers to 'atonement money' and Numbers 31 mentions jewelry being offered for atonement. The prophets indicated clearly that God did not want blood sacrifices, and the rabbis have taught that God is satisfied today with prayer, repentance and good deeds."

Until the Temple was destroyed in A.D. 70, Jewish teaching emphasized the necessity of blood atonement. According to the Talmud, "There is not atonement *(kapparah)* without the blood" (Yoma 5a; Zebahim 6a; Menahot 93b). It is recognized by Jewish and Christian scholars alike that the New Covenant emphasis on

139

blood atonement is based on *Jewish* beliefs of the day. And, although many Jews today think that it is the New Covenant writers who cited Leviticus 17:11 to prove that God required blood atonement, it is actually the *rabbis* of the Talmud who quoted this verse in this way! They recognized that because "the life of a creature is in the blood" God gave it upon the altar to make atonement for His people (*"It is the blood that makes atonement for one's life"* Lev. 17:11).

Blood sacrifices formed the main part of the ancient Israelite Temple service, and, according to Leviticus 16, on the Day of Atonement (Yom Kippur) *the Holy Place itself,* as well as the High Priest and all the people of Israel, were to be cleansed by the *blood* of a sacrificial goat. On the eve of Israel's exodus from Egypt, it was the *blood* of the Passover (*pesach*) lamb, put upon the two doorposts and lintel of the house, that would be a sign to the destroying angel, and the LORD said, "And when I see the *blood,* I will pass over you" (Ex. 12:13). Even the giving of the Torah at Mount Sinai was ratified with the shedding of *blood* ("This is *the blood of the covenant* that the LORD has made with you in accordance with all these words" — Ex. 24:8, and the Aramaic Targum to this verse reads: "And Moses took the blood and poured it on the altar *as atonement for the people ...").*

It is with good reason that the Letter to the Hebrews says that "the law requires that nearly everything be cleansed with blood, *and without the shedding of blood there is no forgiveness"* (Heb. 9:22), since the central importance of the blood, and, in particular, the blood of atonement, is clearly seen in the Tanakh. Any other system of atonement which does not include the blood is not biblical, and any other system of atonement which fails to offer *substitutionary* atonement, i.e., an innocent sacrificial victim dying on behalf of a guilty sinner, is not able to provide real forgiveness of sins.

How then do we account for references to flour offerings and "atonement money" in the Torah? The answers again are simple. According to Leviticus 5:11-13, a poor Israelite who was unable to bring the required trespass offering of a lamb, goat, turtledoves or pigeons could bring instead an offering of fine flour. According to verse 12, the priest will "take a handful of it [i.e., the flour] as a memorial portion, *and burn it on the altar on top of the offerings made to the LORD by fire.*" Then (verse 13) "the priest will make atonement for him." In other words, the priest, in his capacity as mediator for the people, *and having mingled the flour with the blood which was already upon the altar,* would make atonement for his fellow Israelite. Nowhere is it written that "the flour will make atonement," or that "the life of a creature is in the flour." Rather, the whole basis for atonement remained in the sacrificial blood which was upon the altar.

The references to "atonement money" actually have nothing to do with atonement for sins. One example is found in Exodus 30:11-16, where every male Israelite who was to be counted in the census was to pay a *kopher* ("a ransom"; see Ex. 21:30 — the owner of a goring ox that killed a man would have to pay a *kopher,* i.e., a fixed amount of ransom money). Since the taking of a census was considered to be a dangerous enterprise (according to 2 Sam. 24, when David numbered Israel, a plague broke out among the people), God told the Israelites to contribute an offering to the Tabernacle, *so that no plague would break out among them.*

Thus, the *kopher* here had to do with *protection from a plague,* and not forgiveness of sins or personal atonement. In fact, the expression in verse 15 "to atone for your lives" should really be translated as "to pay a *kopher* (ransom) for your souls." This is also the best way to translate Numbers 31:50, since the reference to the children of Israel offering gold jewelry to the LORD again has nothing to do with atonement. Having just counted the soldiers who had gone into battle with Midian (again, they had taken a *census*!), the officers decided to offer some of the spoil to God and thus to pay a *kopher* for their souls. What connection is there between any of these narratives and the concept of personal atonement or forgiveness of sins?

As to the belief that "the prophets indicate clearly that God doesn't want blood sacrifices," it is clear from reading the prophets' own words that what they really opposed were empty sacrifices and *vain* offerings. If one wishes to say that the prophets wanted to *abolish* the sacrificial system, then one would also have to say that the prophets wanted to abolish the Sabbath! (See Is. 1:13: "Stop bringing *meaningless offerings*! . . . New Moons, Sabbaths, and convocations — I cannot bear your evil assemblies.")

The prophets taught that sacrifices without mercy and justice were vain, and that bringing an offering without a repentant and contrite heart was unacceptable. Both of these themes are constantly reiterated in the New Covenant, and one of Yeshua's favorite texts was Hosea 6:6: "For I desire mercy, not sacrifice, and acknowledgement of God rather than burnt offerings" (see, e.g., Matt. 12:7). In fact, when Yeshua gave the Great Commission, He said that *"repentance and forgiveness of sins* will be preached in his name to all nations . . ." (Luke 24:47). Without repentance, the sacrifice of Yeshua will do the sinner no good.

When the Temple was destroyed in A.D. 70, the rabbis instituted what they thought were other forms of atonement, such as prayer, good deeds and charity. They found support for this in verses such as Hosea 14:2 (verse 3 in some versions), which states poetically, "That we may offer the fruit of our lips." Yet, while the Bible sometimes describes prayer, repentance and worship with "sacrifice imagery," it never implies that these things were to take the place of the sacrifices themselves.

Thus, in Psalm 51, after stating that "the sacrifices of God are a broken spirit" (v. 17), David says: "Then there will be righteous sacrifices, whole burnt offerings to delight you; then bulls will be offered on your altar" (v. 19). Another good example is Psalm 141, where David asks that *his prayer* be set before God as *incense*, and that the *lifting up of his hands* be as the *evening sacrifice*. Yet no one would suggest that King David, who brought the ark of God to Jerusalem, and who desired to build a permanent "house" for the LORD, wanted to abolish incense or the evening sacrifice!

The rabbis have taught us much that is beautiful regarding prayer, repentance and good deeds. Yet, as beautiful as this teaching is, it provides us with no suitable replacement for the blood of atonement. To this very day, there are still Orthodox Jews who, recognizing their need for an atonement sacrifice, kill a chicken on Yom Kippur, wave it around their heads and say: "This is my substitute! This is my atonement!" What a sad testimony to our people's lack of true forgiveness outside of God's way through

Messiah! And what clear evidence of the fact that, with the Temple destroyed, traditional Judaism offers no new covenant, *ratified with blood*, and acceptable in the sight of God.

"What did the Jews living in Babylonian exile, before Yeshua died and with no sacrifices to offer, do for atonement?"

It is significant that the Jews who were in exile in Babylon longed for the days when the Temple would be rebuilt, and they fully recognized that it was *because of their sin* that the Temple had been destroyed (see Dan. 9:1-19). Interestingly enough, scholars believe that it was during this very time of exile that the teaching of Isaiah's *Suffering Servant* came to prominence. The hope of the Messiah was coming alive, and the Jewish people were being directed to the One Who would bring to fulfillment the system of Old Covenant blood sacrifices by offering up Himself. By the time the Second Temple was destroyed in A.D. 70, He had already come and done His work.

The Jews in Babylonian captivity could look forward to the coming of the Deliverer Who would be cut "off, but not for himself" (Dan. 9:26, text note). Today, our Jewish people can look back to the One Who paid the ransom for our souls.

"Even if we admit that we need the blood, we still can't believe in Yeshua. God wanted the blood of a goat or a lamb, not a person."

The writer to the Hebrews stated that "it is impossible for the blood of bulls and goats to take away sins" (Heb. 10:4). Obviously a just God could not accept the death of an innocent and ignorant animal for the payment of human sins. Rather, as Rashi stated in his commentary on Leviticus 17:11, there was a principle involved:

Because the life of the flesh of every creature is dependent on the blood, I have therefore given it [upon the altar] to make atonement for the life of man. Let life come and atone for life!

God was teaching His people that sin deserved death (see Deut. 24:16, 30:15, and Ezek. 18:4). Yet, because He was merciful and compassionate, He provided a way of escape — the life of an innocent victim would take the place of the sinner. Passages such as Isaiah 53 make it clear, however, that these sacrifices were only a great object lesson pointing forward to the coming of the One Who would "do away with sin by the sacrifice of himself" (Heb. 9:26). His blood alone would provide an acceptable sacrifice for the sins of the world.

On the holiest day of the year, Yom Kippur, the High Priest would perform a very significant ritual. He would take two goats and present them before the LORD (Lev. 16:7). One goat was to be killed, and its blood offered to *"make atonement for the Most Holy Place because of the uncleanness and rebellion of the Israelites, whatever their sins have been"* (verse 16). Then he would take the second goat, which was still alive, and, laying both his hands on its head, he would *"confess over it all the wickedness and rebellion of the Israelites — all their sins — and put them on the goat's head"* (verse 21). He would then send it away into the wilderness, where the goat would *"carry on itself all their sins to a solitary place"* (verse 22).

God had devised a plan whereby sin would not only be *atoned for*, but it would actually be *removed*. Justice would then be

145

satisfied, for sin would be punished. And yet mercy would be fulfilled, for the sinner would be forgiven. Thus, in physically graphic and literal terms, the LORD was pointing forward to the death of Messiah, Who, in one act, would provide the blood of atonement and remove our sins far from us.

And it is this very concept, viz., *that the suffering of the righteous could provide atonement for the sins of the world,* which is so well known in Judaism. Thus, the Zohar states so clearly that, because "the children of the world are members of one another, when the Holy One desires to give healing to the world, He smites one just man amongst them, and for his sake heals all the rest. Whence do we learn this? From the saying, 'He was wounded for our transgressions, bruised for our iniquities,' i.e., by the letting of his blood — as when a man bleeds his arm — there was healing for us — for all the members of the body. In general a just person is only smitten in order to procure healing and atonement for a whole generation." Could one ask for a clearer statement of the substitutionary death of Yeshua, by Whose wounds we are healed?

The Law (Torah)

"The Torah is forever, every jot and tittle, and only traditional Jews keep it. In fact, even the so-called New Covenant of Jeremiah 31 says that God will put the Torah in our hearts. Therefore, since Yeshua abolished the Torah, He cannot be the Messiah."

Yeshua came to *fulfill* the Torah, not to abolish it, and in Him alone can it truly be said that "the Torah is forever." The clearest example of this truth is found with regard to the rituals of the

Tabernacle and the Levitical priesthood, which formed such a large part of the Mosaic legislation. Over and over it was stated that these institutions and their governing laws were "eternal" (see, e.g., Ex. 27:21, 28:43, 29:9, 29:28, 40:15). But with the Temple destroyed, how could the Jewish people observe these commandments? Without a sanctuary, how could there be legitimate sacrifices, acceptable to God?

The New Covenant provides the answer, for not only did Yeshua foretell the destruction of the Temple forty years in advance (see, e.g., Luke 19:42-44), but, by His substitutionary death on the cross, He fulfilled the demands of the Law's sacrificial system. When the Temple did in fact fall, the followers of Yeshua had no problem, *since they did not have to invent alternative means of atonement.* Their sacrifice for sins had already been made.

As far as traditional Judaism is concerned, it has had no sacrifices since A.D. 70; but those who recognize Yeshua as Messiah have enjoyed His once-for-all sacrifice for every generation. Thus, rather than Yeshua *abolishing* the sacrificial system, He has brought it to fulfillment. In the same way, His identification as the Lamb of God has effectively deepened and underscored the Passover message of liberation from bondage, and Messianic Jews can celebrate this holiday with greater fervor and conviction than ever before. Through Moses they have been delivered from the hand of Pharaoh, and through Yeshua they have been redeemed from the power of sin!

Another example is seen in the fact that the *priesthood of all Israel* was established as a goal of the Torah (Ex. 19:6). The Pharisees sought to realize this goal by developing a system that required every Jew to live with the same ritual cleanliness as a consecrated priest. Unfortunately, this only resulted in new regulations and laws, without bringing the people into a truly priestly ministry. Yet now, through Yeshua the Messiah, all New Covenant believers are "being built into a spiritual house to be *a holy priesthood, offering spiritual sacrifices acceptable to God...*" (1 Pet. 2:5). The New Covenant community has become the very Temple of God (see Eph. 2:19-22), and *every believing member* has direct access into the holy presence of the King!

As far as the *ethical* commandments of the Law are concerned, Yeshua always brought out the *deepest* meanings of God's righteous requirements, and He refused to allow following the LORD to degenerate into a mere outward formality. One of the key features of the New Covenant as prophesied by Jeremiah was that the Torah would be written in our *hearts.* Thus, rather than destroying and nullifying the Law, Yeshua planted it in our hearts and gave us the ability through the Spirit not only to hear, but also to obey.

As for the argument that while Yeshua did not actually abolish the Law, He did *change* it, the question may be asked, "Doesn't Jewish tradition teach that when Messiah comes, He will give new commandments or a new Torah?" In other words, while the righteous principles of the Law will never change, won't some of the earthbound regulations be affected? And if this is possible, could not Yeshua *as Messiah* institute certain "New Commandments," since He had brought about the fulfillment of Torah's demands in His perfect life and sacrificial death? This being the case, is it even accurate to speak of Yeshua's *changing* the Law?

Paul, James and the other early followers of Yeshua were known as observant Jews who were zealous for the Law (Acts 21:20-25). What better proof could there be that Yeshua *in no way* sought to contradict, nullify, or abrogate the commandments of God? It is ironic that today, when Messianic Jews want to worship on Saturday, celebrate the feasts and circumcise their sons as children of Abraham, they are called deceptive and hypocritical!

While there are some who argue that in order for Jeremiah's New Covenant prophecy to be truly fulfilled, God would have to place the *whole Torah* in our hearts, this argument is based on a misconception of the biblical meaning of Torah. Actually, although the Hebrew word *torah* is generally taken as referring to the first Five Books of the Bible (the Pentateuch), and while many Jews understand every reference to *torah* in the Scriptures as meaning *God's entire revelation to His Jewish people,* the fact is that *torah* has a variety of meanings in the Tanakh.

In the sense of "*the* Torah," it can be a synonym for the first Five Books. Yet, more often than not, it simply means "teaching," "instruction," "law," or "regulation." Therefore, when Jeremiah prophesied that under the New Covenant God would put the *Torah* in the hearts of Israel and Judah, he was saying that God's teaching would be planted within the believer, and that the revelation of the LORD would, by the Spirit (see Ezek. 36:25-27), be internalized. He was not saying that *the traditional Jewish Torah,* consisting of Mishnah and Talmud, would automatically be placed in the hearts of the partakers of this covenant!

Such a concept would not only have been strange to Jeremiah's ears, it would have been totally alien, since the concept of "traditional interpretation of the Law" had not even come into existence!

149

And, although traditional Jews claim that the "oral law" was revealed to Moses, almost all modern Jewish scholars will admit that the vast part of the oral law did not even exist before the days of Yeshua. It is therefore with every right that Messianic Jews claim to be the true heirs of Moses and the Prophets, children of the New Covenant. We do not lean on later Jewish tradition. We place our feet firmly on the written revelation of God.

"According to the Law, Yeshua was a false prophet, and those who follow Him are guilty of the worst kind of idolatry: making God into a man!"

Deuteronomy 13:1-3 says: "If a prophet, or one who foretells by dreams appears among you and announces to you a miraculous sign or wonder, and if the sign or wonder of which he has spoken takes place, and he says, 'Let us follow other gods' (gods you have not known) 'and let us worship them,' you must not listen to the words of that prophet or dreamer. The LORD your God is testing you to find out whether you love him with all your heart and with all your soul."

According to these criteria, Yeshua can only be classified as a true and faithful prophet, since the entire object of His earthly ministry was to bring glory and honor to His Father, the God of Israel. When asked which was the first and greatest commandment, Jesus answered: "The most important one . . . is this: 'Hear, O Israel, the Lord our God, the Lord is one. Love the Lord your God with all your heart and with all your soul and with all your mind and with all your strength' " (Mark 12:29-30). Matthew records that when the crowds saw the great miracles He did, "they

150

praised the God of Israel" (Matt. 15:31). Over and again, Yeshua pointed the people to God.

How then could it be said that Yeshua Himself was God? And doesn't this in fact make God into man?

First, it should be emphasized that both traditional Jews as well as Messianic Jews would agree that "God is not a man" (Num. 23:19), and that for God in His totality to become man would mean that God would cease to be God. And yet Judaism has often asked the question of how God, Who is an infinite spiritual Being, can come into fellowship with man, who is a finite physical (and spiritual) being. In answer to this question, various streams of Jewish teaching have offered some different solutions, and yet all of them have this one thought in common: one way or another, God condescended to the level of man.

Some rabbis taught that God, the perfect Spirit, reached down to man, the imperfect earthling, by means of successive emanations (Hebrew *sephirot*) of His being. In other words, He revealed Himself in successive stages or spheres, until, at the lowest sphere, He was able to be perceived by man. Others believed that He revealed Himself to man through His Divine Word (Aramaic *memra'*).

Each of these concepts gives us insights into the New Covenant portrayal of Yeshua as Son of Man and Son of God. First, the idea that there are different spheres or emanations in God is *similar* to the idea of the Trinity: God, Who is One, exists in the Persons of the Father, Son, and Holy Spirit. It is in this way alone that He reveals Himself to man. Thus, Yeshua (the Son) came down to earth to reveal the Father to the world. This is what He meant when

151

He said, "I came from the Father and entered the world: now I am leaving the world and going back to the Father" (John 16:28); and, "No one knows the Father except the Son and those to whom the Son chooses to reveal him" (Matt. 11:27).

There is also much Jewish teaching that speaks of the Shekinah, *the Divine Presence itself,* going into exile with the Jewish people. According to this concept, God cannot be "whole" again until His people return from their physical and spiritual exile, since the rabbis saw in the Shekinah the "motherly" aspect of God, suffering with her children in foreign lands. Similarly, the New Covenant teaches us that God, in the Person of the Son, has joined Himself with man — Yeshua is thus wholly God and wholly man. As the Son, the One Who proceeded forth from the Father, He was the "image of the invisible God" to us. As Man, He lived a perfectly righteous life and died for our sins, thereby becoming the "new" or "second" Adam.

As for the revelation of God by means of His *memra'* (Word), Jewish teaching understands that, because God is infinite and totally above man, He can only interact with us by His Word. Thus, rather than God Himself "touching" this earth, He does it by means of His *memra'. Of course, readers of the New Covenant will immediately think of John's description of Yeshua as "the Word" (Greek, logos)* Who was *with* God in the beginning, and yet at the same time *was* God. And, although "no one has ever seen God, . . . God the One and Only, who is at the Father's side," has declared God to us (John 1:18). We learn about the Father by means of His Word! And, just as the Hebrew Scriptures declare that God created all things *by His Word* (see Gen. 1 and Ps. 33:6-9), so also the New

Covenant teaches us that it is through Yeshua that all things were created, and it is by Him that all things consist (Col. 1:16, 17).

From all this we can learn two important facts. First, while Judaism has consistently taught that God alone is the Savior, it has also taught that, in a sense, "man must save himself." Both of these concepts, rooted as they are in the Scriptures, are fulfilled in Yeshua: as man, He broke the power of sin over man and paid the penalty for our disobedience; as God, He alone is the means by which we can be saved, since man without God will always turn away.

Second, although the New Covenant concept of the Trinity does *not* allow for different *levels* of deity (although the Jewish mystical concept of the *sephirot* seems to view the divine "emanations" in this way), the consistent emphasis in the Scriptures is that the *Father* is God and *Yeshua* is the Messiah. Thus, Paul could write that when all things are made subject to Yeshua the Son, "then the Son himself will be made subject to him who put everything under him, so that God may be all in all" (1 Cor. 15:28).

It is clear, then, that, rather than having a coarse and idolatrous view of God, the New Covenant has explained to us the real way by which God could remain the high and lofty Holy One, sitting on His heavenly throne, while at the same time, as the Savior of the world, He was reaching down to the lowliest sinner. And it is through the earthly ministry of Yeshua that countless millions of people around the world have "*turned to God from idols to serve the living and true God*" (1 Thess. 1:9). He alone is the Savior, and He alone will bring the nations to God.

CHAPTER TWENTY:

KEYS TO UNDERSTANDING MESSIANIC PROPHECY

by Dr. Michael Brown

"You don't know what you're talking about!"

"You're completely misinterpreting Isaiah!"

"This verse has absolutely *nothing* to do with your Jesus! The fact is, it's not even a Messianic prophecy!"

"As for the *real* Messianic prophecies, Jesus fulfilled none of them."

Have you ever had these arguments thrown out at you? Do you know how to answer them? Here are some important keys and principles that will help you to see that, in fact, Yeshua fulfilled the prophecies of the Hebrew Scriptures.

1) Messianic prophecies are not clearly identified as such.

There is not a single verse in the entire Hebrew Bible that is specifically identified as a Messianic prophecy. Nowhere do the Scriptures say, "The next paragraph contains a prediction of the Messiah!" Thus, whether or not one accepts a certain passage as Messianic depends largely on how one understands the person and work of the Messiah.

For example, if someone believes that the Messiah will be a king who will bring peace to the earth, he will probably interpret Isaiah 11 as a Messianic prophecy. But he will not interpret Isaiah 53 in a Messianic way *because it does not fit his preconceived notion of what the Messiah will do.* And so, when we point to Isaiah 53, he will confidently say to us, "But that is not a Messianic prophecy!"

How can we answer his argument? Just ask a simple question: "Who says Isaiah 53 is *not* Messianic while Isaiah 11 *is* Messianic? Who says your interpretation is right?" In other words, help him to see that his understanding of Messianic prophecy is based on *traditional bias* as opposed to *objective scriptural truth.* Thus, rather than being put on the defensive (isn't this where we often end up?), we can challenge his objectivity. Maybe it is he who has brought preconceived notions to the text. If he is open to dialogue, you can take things a step further and ask, "Are you sure your picture of the Messiah is correct? Maybe you are missing some of the pieces to the puzzle! How do you know that Messiah hasn't already come?" And from there you can show him the way!

2) The Messianic hope in Israel developed gradually.

This helps to explain why Messianic prophecies were not clearly identified as such: because they were not initially understood as referring to *the Messiah*. Also, the Hebrew word *mashiach* (Messiah), which literally means "anointed one," almost never refers to *the Messiah* in the Hebrew Bible. Instead, it refers to the anointed king (like Saul or David), the anointed high priest (like Aaron), or even an "anointed" (chosen) foreign ruler (like Cyrus).

Let's apply this to the Messianic hope in Israel. David was a great king, a *mashiach* of the LORD; so was his son Solomon, who had a wonderful reign of peace. Many of the Psalms were written for them or about them: Psalm 72, which is a prayer for Solomon; Psalm 2, which celebrates the coronation of the king; or Psalm 45, which commemorates the royal wedding ceremony. And when all was well, God's people recognized no need for *the Messiah*.

But when Israel's kings began to fail, when there were no more Davids or Solomons, and when the Jewish people were exiled from their Land, they began to realize their need for a special *mashiach*, supernaturally anointed by God. And what do you think happened when they went back and re-read the Psalms? They began to see the Messianic significance of the verses! They recognized, for example, that Psalm 2, which prophesied *the worldwide dominion* of the LORD's anointed, was *not* fulfilled by David, Solomon or any other king. It could only be fulfilled by *the Messiah*. And so, little by little, they began to understand the Messianic hope.

3) Many biblical prophecies are fulfilled gradually.

This key principle applies to *all types* of prophecy, whether Messianic or not. This is also implied by the word "fulfill": the prophet's words had to be "filled up to the full" to be "fulfilled."

Ezekiel, *living in the Babylonian exile*, prophesied that his people should return from their captivity. The fulfillment *began* in 538 B.C.E., when the first group of exiles returned to Judah; it has *continued* in this century with the return of the Jewish people to the Land; and it *will reach fulfillment* when Jesus comes back and gathers His scattered people from every corner of the globe. Over 2500 years and still being fulfilled!

Now let's look at a Messianic prophecy. Zechariah prophesies that when Israel's King comes, He will be "righteous and having salvation, gentle and riding on a donkey. . . . His rule will extend from sea to sea, and from the River to the ends of the earth" (9:9-10). If you show this to a rabbi, he will probably say, "It's clear that Jesus hasn't fulfilled it!"

How should you respond? Simply explain to him that the prophecy *is presently being fulfilled* (i.e., it is in the ongoing process of fully coming to pass): Jesus *came* as the prophet foretold, "righteous and having salvation, gentle and riding on a donkey"; *every day* the number of individuals over whom He reigns as King continues to increase (countless millions from every country!) and *in the future*, when He returns, He will completely establish His rule.

4) The prophets saw the Messiah coming on the immediate horizon of history.

Have you ever stood on top of a mountain and looked across to another mountain peak? The mountains appear to be next to each other, even though there is a huge valley in between. It is the same with biblical prophecy. *The prophets saw the future through a telescope.* Things far away in time appeared close. They did not realize that centuries would come and go between their initial prediction and its actual fulfillment. In fact, to the prophets, the expression "at the end of days" could have meant "right around the corner"!

Why is this principle important to understand with regard to Messianic prophecy? Because we are often accused of taking a verse "out of context." We are told, "That prophecy applied to Isaiah's day 2700 years ago. It certainly does not refer to Jesus!" But did it *really* apply to Isaiah's day, or was it an example of prophecy being telescopic? Did Isaiah see the coming of the Messiah (i.e., a great deliverer) *in the context of his very own day?*

Let's look at Isaiah 9:1-7 (8:23-9:6 in some Bibles), where it is predicted that the yoke of the enemy (i.e., Assyria) would be broken by the son of David *who was already born.* And this son of David would have an everlasting kingdom of peace. When was Assyria crushed? 2600 years ago. Who was born shortly before that time? Hezekiah. Did he *fulfill* the prophecy? Obviously not! But the prophet saw the coming of the future Davidic ruler as if it were about to happen in his very own day.

Watch carefully for prophecies like this, since they are extremely common. In fact, this key to prophetic interpretation is really a summary of the first three principles just given. If you go back and read them again, things will begin to fall into place for you.

5) It is important to read every prophecy in its overall context in Scripture.

Do the New Covenant writers take Old Covenant verses out of context, or are they faithful to the meaning of the text? In Matthew 1:23, Isaiah 7:14 is applied to the birth of Jesus (the virgin [or, maiden] will bear a son and call his name Immanuel). But is this quotation faithful to Isaiah? How can Matthew apply *a sign given to King Ahaz about 734 B.C.E.* to the birth of Yeshua over 700 years later? How could this be a relevant sign?

Consider the context of Isaiah chapters 7-11. Judah was being attacked by Israel and Aram. These nations wanted to replace Ahaz, who represented the house of David (see Is. 7:2, 13), with their own man named Ben Tabeel. *This would mean the end of Davidic rule in Judah.* Yet when Ahaz would not ask God for a sign, God gave him His own: a child named Immanuel (meaning "God is with us") would be born and within a few years, before the child was very old, Judah's enemies would be destroyed.

Who was this Immanuel? Obviously a child to be born to the house of David in place of faithless Ahaz, a son who would be a token of the fact that God was with His people (in other words, good news for the nation and bad news for Ahaz!). But is his birth ever mentioned in the book of Isaiah? No! In fact, the birth of Isaiah's son Maher-Shalal-Hash-Baz in Isaiah 8:1-4 *seems to take its place as a time-setter* (read Is. 7:14-16 and 8:3-4; before Maher-Shalal-Hash-Baz would be very old, Judah's enemies would be destroyed — just what was said about Immanuel!).

What happened to Immanuel? Nothing is clearly said. But what is clearly said in Isaiah 9:6-7 (9:5-6 in some Bibles) and 11:1-16 is that there will come forth a rod from Jesse (David's father) who will rule the nations in righteousness.

And this was Matthew's context! He was reading Isaiah 7-11 in full! Thus he quotes Isaiah 7:14 in Matthew 1:23; Isaiah 9:1-2 (8:23-9:1 in some Bibles) in Matthew 4:15-16; and he alludes to Isaiah 11:1 in Matthew 2:23 (the Hebrew word for "Nazarene" resembles the Hebrew word for "branch").

Was anyone born in Isaiah's day that began to fulfill the Immanuel prophecy? We simply do not know. But of this we can be sure: Jesus, the ideal King from the house of David, and clearly the subject of the Messianic prophecies in chapters 9 and 11, is Immanuel — God with us — in the fullest sense of the word!

6) The Messiah was to be both a Priest and King.

Everyone who believes in the Messiah accepts the *royal* prophecies of the Scriptures as referring to Messiah the King. But what about the predictions of *suffering?* What do *these* verses have to do with the Messiah?

Here is an important answer! *The prophecies of suffering and death point to the priestly ministry of the Messiah, since it was the duty of the High Priest to intercede for his people and make atonement for their sins.*

Did you know that in the first century of this era there was widespread belief in the coming of a *priestly* Messianic figure as well as a *royal* Messianic figure? This belief was almost correct. There *was* to be a priest and there was to be a king, only these two figures were one! According to Psalm 110, the Davidic ruler was to be both priest and king. In Zechariah 6, *the crown* is placed on the head *of the High Priest* named Joshua (he is also called *Yeshua* in Ezra and Nehemiah!), who is then referred to as "the Branch," a Messianic title!

Thus, it is clear that the Messiah would have a dual role: as High Priest He would take His people's sins on Himself and intercede for them; as King He would rule and reign. Because traditional Judaism has largely forgotten the Messiah's priestly work, it has not always recognized key passages in Isaiah as referring to Him.

7) The Messiah is the ideal representative of His people.

In ancient Israel, the king and his people were one. As the kings of Israel went, so went the nation. They saw themselves represented in their head.

How does this apply to the Messiah? First, the history of Israel paralleled the life of Jesus. For example, when Moses was born, Pharaoh was trying to kill Israelite baby boys, and when Jesus was born, Herod began killing Jewish baby boys. Also, both the nation of Israel as well as Jesus spent their early years in Egypt. (*That* is why Matthew quotes Hos. 11:1 in Matt. 2:15! Compare also Matt. 2:20 with Ex. 4:19.)

And because the Messiah was the ideal representative of His people, *He fulfills the words of their psalms.* Thus Psalm 22, the psalm of the righteous sufferer whom God wonderfully delivers, is not identified at all as a Messianic prophecy. Yet, to any impartial reader, it is clear that both the depth of suffering described as well as the universal effects of the deliverance can refer

162

only to Jesus, the ideal righteous Sufferer, the representative King, the greater David. Therefore, the New Covenant writers often see the Psalms as containing Messianic prophecies, since the Messiah is seen as their ultimate, representative subject.

* * * *

How can you put all these principles together? Every time you see a Messianic prophecy quoted in the New Covenant, look it up in the Old Covenant and read the whole section from which it is taken (this could be a paragraph, a chapter or even more). Then, try and see which of the interpretive keys explains the quote. Remember: many times several principles are at work together!

Not only will you enrich your understanding of the Word, but you will learn to appreciate how wonderfully God has woven together the prophecies of the Messiah's coming.

And *then* what should you do? Share your discoveries with an interested Jewish friend!

CHAPTER TWENTY-ONE:

DOCTRINES OF JUDAISM

by Louis Goldberg

Reprinted from *Our Jewish Friends*, with the permission of
Loizeaux Brothers publishers

Note: The Orthodox and Conservative beliefs are shown together because the two groups hold the same basic doctrines,
although they differ in their practice of Judaism.

	ORTHODOX AND CONSERVATIVE	REFORM
SCRIPTURES	Are given great emphasis and regarded as from God (Maimonides, Principles 6-9).	Are not verbally inspired in Bible sense.

	Torah is inspired in degrees.	Torah has errors but does stress an ethic and derives a moral.
ORAL LAW	Is the traditional understanding of the Scriptures and is stressed.	Is highly regarded but not considered authoritative. Is questioned through rational approach.
GOD	Concept is based upon Deuteronomy 6:4 (Maimonides, Principles 1-5).	Is regarded in monotheistic way; has great emphasis. (But is the belief personal?)
1) Triune Nature of God	Is denied.	Is denied.
2) Holy Spirit	Is recognized.	Their understanding varies.
MAN		
1) Nature	Has good and evil bent.	Has divine spark.
2) Potential	Is greatly emphasized.	Is stressed.
3) Fall	Death is a result of Adam's sin, but there is no original sin.	Not accepted; man is a product of evolution.

SIN	Is given great emphasis. Horizontal stress (man to man) is major. Some vertical aspects (man to God) are present.	Is recognized. Social aspects are emphasized.
SALVATION (Jewish Idea)	Is given strong emphasis. The great three are essential: Prayer — Tefillah Good Works — Mitzvot Repentance — Teshuvah Suffering has merit.	Is seen as the social emphasis for this life.
MESSIAH	Is regarded as personal. Is seen as human or superhuman (but not God). Many Conservative believe as the Reform.	Personal Messiah is denied. They are looking for Messianic golden age.
MESSIANIC KINGDOM	Has strong emphasis. Day of judgment of the nations is to come.	Is denied. Most are interested in fitting into current culture, but some have second thoughts.

	Messiah will rectify all injustices.	
	Israel will be at the head of nations.	
ESCHATOLOGY **(Study of** **end-times)**	Has little emphasis. It is more important to learn how to live here and now.	Has little emphasis.
		Death ends all except memory of the departed in the living.
	There are so many opinions that it is hard to define an ordered eschatology.	
1) Intermediate State*	Righteous have their place in Garden of Eden in Sheol.	
	Unrighteous have their place in Gehena.	
2) Resurrection	Some rabbis indicate a universal one.	
	Some say only Israel.	
	Some say only the righteous.	
	It is seen as physical.	

*The time period between death and resurrection.

Some believe the body will be the same body which was buried.

Others say that it will be renewed but not glorified.

3) Ultimate State

Righteous will enjoy God in the Garden of Eden.

For the unrighteous there are different ideas:

a) suffering, then all saved (most rabbis believe this).

b) suffering, then annihilation.

c) suffering forever.

CHAPTER TWENTY-TWO:

GLOSSARY OF MAJOR RABBINIC WRITINGS AND TERMS

Aggada — *See Haggada.*

Babylonian Talmud — The foundational text for Jewish religious study, it consists of 2,500,000 words of Hebrew and Aramaic commentary and expansion on the *Mishnah.* It includes much *Halakha* as well as *Haggada,* and thus it touches on virtually every area of life, religion, custom, folklore, and law. It reached its final form between A.D. 500-600, and it is mainly the product of the Babylonian sages. See also *Palestinian Talmud.*

Five Scrolls — (Hebrew, *kha-MESH me-gi-LOT*) The biblical books of Song of Songs (Song of Solomon), Ruth, Lamentations, Ecclesiastes and Esther. They were read in the synagogues on special holidays. See also *Ketuvim.*

Haggada — (Sometimes spelled *Aggada*) Non-legal (i.e., non-binding) rabbinic stories, sermons and commentaries relating to the *Tanakh* and Jewish life. See also *Halakha* and *Midrash*.

Halakha — A specific legal ruling ("What is the *halakha* in this case?"), or rabbinic legal material in general. The word *Halakha* is interpreted as meaning "the way to go." See also *Haggada*.

Humash — (Pronounced KHU-mash) Another name for the Five Books of Moses (see also *Written Torah*).

Ibn Ezra — Abraham Ibn Ezra (1089-1164). He was one of the three greatest Jewish medieval biblical commentators, especially famous for his careful attention to Hebrew grammar. See also *Radak* and *Rashi*.

Jerusalem Talmud — See *Palestinian Talmud*.

Kabbalah — The general term for Jewish mystical writings and traditions. It literally means "that which has been received." See also *Zohar*.

Ketuvim — Writings. This refers to the third division of the Hebrew Bible (see *Tanakh*) and includes Psalms, Proverbs, Job, the *Five Scrolls*, Daniel, Ezra-Nehemiah and 1-2 Chronicles.

Masoretic Text — The term for the closely related Hebrew text editions of the *Tanakh* transmitted by the Masoretes ("transmitters") from the 6th to the 11th centuries. All translations of the *Tanakh* (including the King James and *all* modern versions) are primarily based on this text. (Note: there is not one Masoretic Bible. There are thousands of Masoretic manuscripts with almost identical texts.)

172

Midrash — Rabbinic commentaries on a verse, chapter or whole book of the *Tanakh*, marked by creativity and interpretive skill. The best-known collection is called *Midrash Rabba*, covering the Five Books of Moses as well as the *Five Scrolls*.

Mishnah — The first written collection of legal material relating to the laws of the *Torah* and the ordinances of the sages. It provides the starting point for all subsequent *Halakha*. It was compiled about A.D. 200 by Rabbi Judah HaNasi (the Prince) and especially emphasizes the traditions of the rabbis who flourished from A.D. 70-200. See *Talmud* and *Halakha*.

Mishneh Torah — Systematic compilation of all Jewish law by Moses Maimonides (also called Rambam; 1135-1204). It remains a standard legal text to this day. See also *Shulkhan Arukh*.

Mitzvah — Commandment. The foundation of Jewish observance consists of keeping the so-called 613 commandments of the *Torah*.

Nevi'im — Prophets. This refers to the second division of the Hebrew Bible (see *Tanakh*) and consists of Joshua, Judges, 1-2 Samuel, 1-2 Kings (together called the Former Prophets) and Isaiah, Jeremiah, Ezekiel and the Twelve Minor Prophets (together called the Latter Prophets).

Oral Torah — All rabbinic traditions relating to the *Written Torah* and various legal aspects of Jewish life. The traditions were originally passed on orally before they were put into writing.

Palestinian Talmud — Similar to the *Babylonian Talmud* but based primarily on the work of the sages in Israel. It is shorter in scope, less authoritative, and therefore studied less than the

Babylonian Talmud. It reached its final form in the Land of Israel about A.D. 400.

Radak — Acronym for Rabbi David Kimchi (pronounced *kim-KHEE;* 1160-1235). He wrote important commentaries on much of the *Tanakh.* See also *Ibn Ezra* and *Rashi.*

Rashi — Acronym for *R*abbi *Sh*lomo *Y*itschaki (pronounced *yits-KHA-ki;* 1040-1105), the foremost Jewish commentator on the *Tanakh* and *Babylonian Talmud.* Traditional Jews always begin their studies in Bible and Talmud with *Rashi's* commentaries as their main guide. See also *Ibn Ezra* and *Radak.*

Responsa Literature — (Hebrew, *she-ey-LOT u-te-shu-VOT,* "Questions and Answers") A major source of *Halakha* from A.D. 600 until today, it consists of the answers to specific legal questions posed to leading rabbinic authorities in every generation. See also *Oral Law.*

Shulkhan Arukh — The standard and most authoritative Jewish law code, compiled by Rabbi Joseph Karo (1488-1575). See also *Mishneh Torah.*

Talmud — See *Babylonian Talmud* and *Palestinian Talmud (Jerusalem Talmud).*

Targum — Literally, "translation." This refers to the expansive Aramaic translations of the Hebrew Bible which were read in the synagogues where biblical Hebrew was no longer understood. They were put in written form between A.D. 300-1200. The most important *Targums* are *Targum Onkelos* to the Five Books of Moses and *Targum Jonathan* to the *Nevi'im* (Prophets).

174

Tanakh — Acronym for *Torah, Nevi'im, Ketuvim,* the Jewish name for the Old Covenant in its entirety. Although the order of the books is different from that of a Christian Old Covenant, the contents are exactly the same.

Torah — Literally, "teaching, instruction, law." It can refer to: 1) the *Written Torah* (the first division of the Hebrew Bible; see *Tanakh*); or 2) the *Oral Torah* in its entirety (this of course includes the *Written Torah* as well).

Torah She-be-'al-peh — See *Oral Torah.*

Torah She-bikhtav — See *Written Torah.*

Written Torah — The Five Books of Moses (the Pentateuch). See also *Humash.*

Zohar — The foundational book of Jewish mysticism. It was composed in the 13th century, although mystical tradition dates it to the 2nd century. See also *Kabbalah.*

CHAPTER TWENTY-THREE:

THE MEANING AND IMPORTANCE OF THE JEWISH HOLIDAYS

by John Fischer

When God taught the Jewish people His truths in the time of Moses, He communicated them in a unique way. As any good educator or communicator would, He employed vehicles that involved all of our senses in order to leave an indelible impression on us. These vehicles communicate God's message in beautiful, picturesque ways. Most significantly they include the festivals of the Jewish calendar.

A study of Numbers 10:10 reveals that God instituted the festivals and new-month celebrations to serve as reminders of Him and our obligations to Him. As such they serve as teaching aids for absorbing religious truths. They can also serve to communicate God's message to our children and friends.

In Deuteronomy 6:4-9, God commanded us to daily teach our children His ways in all we do. In this way they (and we) will understand that following God is a lifestyle and is relevant to every aspect of life. The observance of the calendar events aids in this process and demonstrates that each day of our lives has tremendous significance before God. Rabbi Samson Hirsch explained it well:

> *"The catechism of the Jew consists of his calendar. On the pinions of time which bear us through life, God has inscribed the eternal words of his soul-inspiring doctrine, making days and weeks, months and years the heralds to proclaim His truths. Nothing would seem more fleeting than these heralds of time, but to them God has entrusted the care of His holy things, thereby rendering them more imperishable and more accessible than any mouth of priest, any monument, temple or altar could have done"* (*Judaism Eternal*, Vol. 1, p. 3).

FULFILLMENT IN THE FESTIVALS

The B'rit Hadasha (New Testament) stresses that Yeshua (Jesus) fulfills the message of these calendar events, providing them with added significance. Hebrews (8:5; 10:1) speaks in terms of them being "shadows of good things that are coming," that is, they highlight the Messiah. But a shadow can't highlight anyone if it's removed from the picture. Therefore, the "shadows" still have important functions to perform.

Yeshua taught (Matt. 5:17-19) that anyone who annulled the least of God's commandments, or taught others to do so, would be called "least" in His kingdom. He didn't come to abolish or set aside the Law and its teachings; He came to do the opposite, to fulfill them. The term Yeshua used for "fulfill" carries the idea of bringing to full expression, showing someone forth in his full radiance. The festivals are beautiful pictures of this.

Although the Sabbath (cf. Lev. 23:2-3) and new-month celebrations are part of the calendar events, the rest of this chapter focuses on the major festivals.

THE CYCLE OF FESTIVALS
AND THEIR FULFILLMENT

Leviticus 23 relates the yearly cycle of Jewish festivals. In addition to the teachings being communicated, the very chronology of these festivals has significance.

PASSOVER WEEK

Pesach

Exodus 12 and the earlier chapters tell the story of Pesach. Nine plagues had not convinced the Pharaoh of Egypt to release the Jewish people. God had one final plague in mind. In order to be protected from this plague, each family had to kill a lamb and apply its blood to the door of their home. When the angel of destruction passed through Egypt, he passed over the homes with blood on the door.

Leviticus 23:4-5 commands this festival to be observed in the *first* month of the Jewish year. Pesach no longer occurs in the first month because the calendar was later changed to correspond to the Babylonian calendar. Notice too, the strong association of Pesach with unleavened bread. Traditionally, Pesach is observed much as it has been since before Yeshua. The major exceptions include the presence of the lamb bone replacing the eating of the lamb, and the addition of the Afikomen (the so-called "dessert").[53]

An incident from the time of the Second Temple highlights the Messianic significance of Pesach. At that time people traveled great distances to observe the holiday in Jerusalem. They would then go to the Temple area to select a lamb for the festival. There the priest would indicate an appropriate lamb by pointing to the animal and saying: "Behold the lamb." On one occasion Yohanan (John the Baptizer), the son of a priest, saw Yeshua coming in the distance, pointed and said: "Look, the Lamb. . . ." But he went on to complete his statement, " . . . the Lamb of God, who takes away the sin of the world" (John 1:29). He thus indicated that Yeshua's forthcoming sacrificial death was related to the meaning of Pesach. Later, Rav Shaul (Apostle Paul) stated, "Yeshua, our Passover lamb, has been sacrificed" (1 Cor. 5:7).

Yeshua the Messiah acted as God's Passover lamb for us; He died that we might live. Before He died, Yeshua took one of the cups of wine during Pesach and said that it represented His blood, which would shortly be shed on our behalf for the forgiveness of sins (Matt. 26:27-28). This would have reminded His followers of the blood of the Passover lamb that was applied to the doorposts back in Egypt.

53. There is ample indication that Yeshua Himself probably instituted this practice, which then found its way into traditional observance because of the early Messianic Jews.

Now, as we celebrate Pesach, we remember not only God's actions during the time of the Exodus, but also Yeshua's death for us, which secured our atonement. In fact, the term used for the piece of matzot which is "hidden" during the Pesach meal, Afikomen — a Greek, not Hebrew, term — literally means "the one who came." It was used in the first couple of centuries as a title of Yeshua the Messiah.[54]

Feast of Unleavened Bread

Leviticus 23:6-8 describes this festival, which is closely connected to Pesach and also uses unleavened bread. Unleavened bread (matzot) may well picture "pure" bread in that it has no yeast-like agents. In this sense it remains "uncontaminated." For this reason, leaven frequently represented evil (1 Cor. 5:6-7). This feast became part of the Passover week observance because of the command to eat matzot for seven days during Pesach (Ex. 12:18).

When Yeshua ate His last Passover meal, He took the matzot, broke it — as we do even today — and said it represented His body, which would be given as a sacrifice for us (Matt. 26:26), hence, the significance of "pure" or unleavened bread.

Ceremony of Firstfruits

According to Leviticus 23:9-14, the ceremony of firstfruits occurs immediately after Pesach. The very first part of the harvest is waved before God, a symbolic way of presenting it to God, "so

54. Cf. Lampe, *A Patristic Greek Lexicon.*

it will be accepted on your behalf" (v. 11). Traditional observance associates this ceremony with Passover week. The beginning of the fifty-day period of counting the omer, observed by traditional Jews, reflects this ceremony today.

Three days after His death and right after Pesach, Yeshua rose from the dead (Matt. 28:1f). Rav Shaul (Apostle Paul) wrote that by rising from the dead, Yeshua became "the *firstfruits* of those who have fallen asleep [died]" (1 Cor. 15:20). Like the firstfruits (Lev. 23:11), His resurrection was "accepted for us" as He was "raised . . . for our justification" (Rom. 4:25). So the ceremony of the firstfruits and its traditional counterpart, the beginning of the counting of the omer, should remind us of Yeshua's resurrection. The resurrection demonstrated that He was indeed the Messiah and that His sacrifice had in fact secured atonement for us.

As we recall the significance of Passover week, we recognize several truths. The blood of the Passover lamb reminds us of Yeshua's great loss of blood at His crucifixion, and the matzot recall His body sacrificed on our behalf. These holidays picture His death. The ceremony of firstfruits pictures His resurrection. Thus, the Messianic significance of Passover week relates to the atonement made for us by Yeshua the Messiah, effected by His death and resurrection.

SHAVUOT

Chronologically, Shavuot (Pentecost), the Feast of Weeks, occurs next in the original Jewish calendar (Lev. 23:15-22). This special time takes place fifty days after the firstfruits ceremony. Along with other offerings, two loaves of leavened bread were presented to God. Deuteronomy 16:9-17 indicates that, although this festival accompanied the harvest, it was intended to remind us that we were once slaves in Egypt, before God set us free.

As our traditions developed, Shavuot became the festival of the giving of the Law. Evidently, the rabbis concluded by calculations that the giving of the Law at Mt. Sinai took place on this day. Traditional Jews read the scroll of Ruth in the synagogue on this day and occasionally refer to Shavuot as "Atzeret shel Pesach," the completion of Passover. Messianic significance abounds in this festival. From God's perspective, the time of great "harvest" — when large numbers of Jews and then Gentiles came into a personal relationship with Him — was initiated at the Shavuot after Yeshua's resurrection (Acts 2:40-43). The two leavened (impure) loaves of Shavuot *may* therefore symbolize Jew and Gentile "presented" to God and now part of His "family." The scroll of Ruth, the story of the Gentile woman who became part of God's people, certainly pictures this time when Gentiles first became God's children in large numbers.

Rav Shaul's (Apostle Paul) teaching about our former conditions as slaves to sin (Rom. 6-8) is certainly reminiscent of Shavuot's reminder that we were formerly slaves in Egypt. God set us free from slavery to sin by placing His Spirit in us to enable us to live as He intended (Rom. 8:1-4). God visibly placed His Spirit (Ruach HaKodesh) in Yeshua's followers on that important Shavuot centuries ago (Acts 2:4).

Technically, the work of atonement is not complete unless man's sin nature ("*yetzer hara,*" evil inclination) has been dealt with and power to overcome it has been granted. The coming of the Ruach HaKodesh served as the completion of Passover (Atzeret shel Pesach), the completion of our atonement, in the sense that through the Spirit God gives us the power we need to overcome our tendency to evil. Yeshua Himself indicated this (John 16:7): "Unless I go away, the Counselor [Ruach HaKodesh] will not come to you; but if I go [*i.e., "firstfruits,"* His resurrection], I will send him to you" (Shavuot, the completion of the fifty days from firstfruits, occurring during Passover week).

Shavuot possesses other Messianic significance as well. God spoke of a time when He would write His laws in our hearts (Jer. 31:32-33). Ezekiel 36:25-27 mentions His placing the Ruach in our hearts in this same connection. So God associates the giving of the Ruach (Acts 2:4; Ezek. 36:25-27) with the placing of His Law in our hearts (Jer. 31:32-33). What more appropriate time to visibly place His Ruach in His people than on Shavuot, the feast of the giving of the Law! Notice that Ezekiel connects the giving of the Ruach with the sprinkling of water on us. Moroccan Jews have an ancient custom they perform on Shavuot. They pour water on each other! (Hayyim Schauss, *Guide to the Jewish Holy Days,* p. 95.) This becomes one more symbol that Shavuot pictures God's visibly placing the Ruach in the followers of Yeshua.

ROSH HASHANAH

This Biblical holiday originated as "a sacred assembly, commemorated with trumpet blasts" (Lev. 23:23-25), a holy gathering. Today, we observe it as the New Year because, according to tradition, God created the world on this day. Rosh Hashanah is frequently called the day of remembrance (Yom haZikaron) or the day of judgment (Yom HaDin) in view of its inauguration of the days of awe. The first name stresses God's faithfulness to His covenant and promises, the second His righteousness and justice. Still, the holiday conveys joy and delight, as illustrated by the custom of eating sweet things (e.g., apples dipped in honey).

A very interesting ceremony, Tashlich, grew up as part of the Rosh Hashanah observance. Devout Jews go to the edge of a body of water and empty their pockets or throw stones into the water. As they do this, they repeat Micah 7:18-20, which includes: "You will ... hurl all our iniquities into the depths of the sea."

Since Rosh Hashanah originated as the memorial of blowing of trumpets, the shofar plays an important role. Among other things it symbolizes, according to the rabbis, God's kingship and the coming of the Messianic Age (Olam Haba).

Rosh Hashanah has deep Messianic significance. The rabbis taught that one day the shofar would sound and the Messiah would come. When He came, the dead would rise (Joseph Hertz, *Daily Prayer Book*, p. 865). About a decade after Yeshua, Rav Shaul (Apostle Paul) talked about this when he referred to the fact that Yeshua would return for His followers and would thereafter rule the earth as Messiah the King. People refer to this event as the Rapture or Yeshua's Second Coming. In describing the Rapture, Rav Shaul (Apostle Paul) said: "For the Lord himself will come down from heaven, with a loud command, with the voice of the archangel and with the trumpet [shofar] call of God, and the dead in Christ will rise first" (1 Thess. 4:16). This day will certainly be characterized by joy, delight, and sweetness (cf. apples dipped in honey).

This particular resurrection is for those who have had, as Tashlich reminds us, their sins thrown into the sea by God because they have accepted Yeshua as Messiah. At this time, we will undergo a new *creation*, so to speak (1 Cor. 15:50-53); we will receive new bodies. Remember, Rosh Hashanah traditionally commemorates the original creation. The Rapture, while being a sign of God's faithfulness to us (Yom HaZikaron, day of remembrance), ushers in a time of judgment on the world (Yom HaDin, day of judgment).

In Leviticus, the term "memorial" does not mean remembering something which is past. It calls attention to something about to occur. As we observe Rosh Hashanah, we should anticipate the time of Yeshua's return.

YOM KIPPUR

The Bible (Lev. 23:26-32) describes this day (the Day of Atonement) as most solemn, a time of introspection and repentance. Those who didn't observe this holy day were severely punished. Only on Yom Kippur could the high priest enter the most sacred part of the sanctuary, and only he could enter. There, after making a sacrifice for himself, he brought the blood from the sacrifice made for the people (Lev. 16). On this day, atonement was made for the *whole* nation, as a goat died in place of the people. (According to the most up-to-date studies, atonement (Hebrew, *"kippur"*) means "ransom by means of a substitute.")

Traditional observance has maintained the solemnity of this great day of repentance. Reminiscences of the Yom Kippur sacrifice still exist among some religious Jews in the custom of Kapporot. A chicken is swung over the head as the following is recited: "This is my substitute, this is my commutation; this chicken goes to death; but may I be gathered and enter into a long and happy life and into peace."

Messianic significance abounds. The services during the period of Rosh Hashanah and Yom Kippur refer repeatedly to the binding or sacrifice of Isaac ("Akedah"). The rabbis teach that in some way God accepts the "sacrifice" of Isaac on our behalf. Isaac beautifully foreshadows the sacrifice of Messiah (e.g., Heb. 11:17-19), whose sacrifice God accepted on our behalf. The Haftorah portion on Yom Kippur is the book of Jonah, the prophet who spent three days in the belly of a large fish before emerging. When Yeshua was challenged to provide evidence for His Messiahship, He pointed to the example of Jonah (Matt. 12:39-40). He used Jonah as a picture of His own death and resurrection. A musaf prayer found in many older Yom Kippur prayer books exhibits additional Messianic significance:

"The Messiah our righteousness has turned from us. We are alarmed, we have no one to justify us. Our sins and the yoke of our transgressions He bore. He was bruised for our iniquities. He

187

carried on His shoulders our sins. With His stripes we are healed. Almighty God, hasten the day that He might come to us anew; that we may hear from Mt. Lebanon a second time through the Messiah" ("Oz M'lifnai B'reshit").

Rav Shaul (Apostle Paul) writes of a time in the future when all Israel will be redeemed and will have atonement (Rom. 11:26). The prophet Zechariah (12:10; 13:9) also predicted this time of national redemption. In the past, atonement was made for *all* Israel on Yom Kippur. Presently, this holy day looks forward to the time when *all* Israel will accept the atonement provided by the Messiah. This will be a time not only of national atonement for Israel but of atonement for the entire world.

As we await this day, we can celebrate Yom Kippur by thanking God for the atonement available through Yeshua and by praying that more of our people will recognize and accept Him as their atonement. The tenor of the day also provides us with an opportunity for self-searching, repentance and recommitment to God (cf. 2 Cor. 13:5; 1 John 1:9).

SUCCOT

The Bible (Lev. 23:43) pictured Succot (Festival of Booths or Tabernacles) as an eight-day period of rejoicing. Although it occurs at harvest time, the festival virtually ignores the harvest theme as it commemorates God's faithfulness to Israel through the wilderness wanderings after they left Egypt.

Traditional observance has maintained the spirit of great rejoicing during Succot. As in biblical times, meals are to be eaten in booths as a "picture of man's sojourn under God's wings," and also as a reminder of freedom from Egypt (Lev. 23:43). Participants carry the lulav branches and the etrog[55] in a procession through the synagogue and wave the branches in four directions. The waving of the branches goes back to earlier times when Near Eastern people welcomed visiting dignitaries in this way.

The seventh day of the celebration, Hoshana Rabba, gets its name from the prayers said on that day. Those prayers begin with the Hebrew "hoshana" ("save now") and include some special Messianic prayers. In tune with the spirit of joy, the participants recite Hallel Psalms (113-118) during the week's celebration. It all culminates in the ninth day with Simchat Torah, the day of rejoicing over God's gift of the Law to the Jewish people.

During Second Temple times, two events that no longer take place highlighted the celebration. Water, drawn from a nearby source, was brought to the Temple and poured out by the altar as Isaiah 12:3 was repeated: "With joy you will draw water from the wells of salvation." The torchlight parade, brilliantly illuminating the Temple at night, stood out as the other great event, possibly reflecting a verse from one of the Hallel Psalms (118:27): "The LORD is God, and he has made his light to shine upon us."

Yeshua chose these two events to highlight His mission as Messiah. As the water was being poured by the altar, He announced: "If anyone is thirsty, let him come to me and drink. Whoever believes in me, as the Scripture has said, streams of living water will flow from within him" (John 7:37-39). As torches lit up the Temple, He shouted: "I am the light of the world. Whoever follows me . . . will have the light of life" (John 8:12).

55. A lemon-like fruit.

Messianic significance also abounds in the celebration as traditionally observed since Temple days. Two verses from one of the Hallel Psalms stand out (118:22-23): "The stone the builders rejected has become the capstone." This beautifully pictures the time when Yeshua will reign as Messiah, the king over the earth. The waving of the lulav, that oriental form of welcome, will be directed toward Him in that day. One of the prayers of Hoshana Rabba echoes this welcome to Messiah.

"A voice heralds, heralds and saith: Turn unto Me and be ye saved, today if ye hear My voice. Behold the man who springs forth, Branch[56] is his name. . . ."

"But to His anointed, the Messiah, He giveth grace. Grant salvation to the eternal people. To David and to His seed[57] forever. . . ."

This prayer eagerly anticipates the coming of the Messianic kingdom. Then, people will rejoice in the presence of the living Torah, Yeshua, the one called the Word of God (cf. John 1:1f). That Simchat Torah will have no rivals in its joy and celebration. Zechariah 14:16-19 describes this as a time when all nations, not just Israel, will keep the festival of Succot and live in booths.

When the Apostle Peter (Shimon HaShaliach) awoke from dozing and for a moment caught sight of the glory Yeshua reflected at His transfiguration, he immediately thought the Messiah had

56. Both are references to Messiah, the seed and branch of David (cf. Is. 9:5-6, Jer. 23:5-6).

57. See footnote above.

come to rule. In the spirit of the Zechariah passage, he appropriately suggested that they begin celebrating Succot (Matt. 17:1-4). His idea was good, but his timing was off. Shimon (Apostle Peter) discovered later that he had had the privilege of looking into the future that Zechariah had predicted. So Succot pictures the coming reign of Messiah over the earth, that time of ultimate freedom.

As we celebrate Succot each year, we can anticipate that time when the booths will no longer picture our present "sojourn under God's wings." *Then* they will remind us of the past, *before* the reign of Yeshua HaMashiach the King. In the meantime, the booths remind us to depend on God and not on material goods (cf. Matt. 6:25-33).

THE HOLIDAYS OUTSIDE THE LEVITICUS CYCLE

Purim

Purim commemorates the events of the scroll of Esther, as we relive our deliverance from Haman and take renewed faith in outliving Hamans of other times. The celebration provides a joyous, carnival-type atmosphere. Men dress up as women, women as men; people playfully snatch each other's food. All of this serves as a picture of disorder.

Haman was the first to attempt to exterminate the Jews, so the holiday is a reminder of God's preservation of and commitment to Israel. But in the context of Purim, it reminds us of God's preservation *during our exile.* The disorderly, raucous, carnival nature of Purim then serves to remind us of God's preservation of our people through the years of exile until Messiah rules and disorder disappears.

Hanukah

Hanukah reminds us of the victory won by the Maccabees in 165 B.C.E. to insure the purity of the worship of God and to preserve the distinctiveness of Israel and Jewish identity. After God granted this tremendous victory, the people cleansed and rededicated the Temple. The Syrian ruler Antiochus had defiled the Temple and turned it into a heathen shrine, hence the need for cleansing. Therefore, Hanukah originated as the festival of the dedication or cleansing of the Temple.

Yeshua used the Feast of Dedication (John 10:22) to proclaim Himself as the Good Shepherd (John 10:1*ff*). In the Jewish writings, shepherds frequently represented the leaders of Israel, both good and bad. (The Maccabees, for example, would have been considered among the good shepherds.) Yeshua, therefore, announced Himself as the Good Shepherd *par excellence.*

The book of Daniel predicted the rise of Antiochus and his defiling of the Temple (Dan. 8 & 11). Daniel also used Antiochus to represent a figure in the future whom Christian theologians call the Antichrist (Antimessiah), who will also defile the Temple (in this case, the Third Temple, which is not yet built). The Antimessiah will cause great persecution for the Jewish people, a time known as Jacob's trouble (Jer. 30:4-7; cf. Zech. 13:8-9). At this time, Yeshua the Messiah, as the great shepherd-leader (Zech. 12-14; cf. 1 Pet. 5:4), will come and win a tremendous victory, greater than that won by Yehudah the Maccabee. He will save Israel and establish His worldwide rule.

Hanukah looks back to a victory and the preservation of the Jewish people when they were *in the land.* For us, it looks forward to a time when our Jewish people will be preserved despite intense suffering. This preservation, again while the Jewish people are in the land, will culminate in the victory won by the Great Shepherd, Yeshua.

Thus, Purim pictures our preservation from our enemies while we're in exile, and Hanukah pictures our preservation while we're in the land. And, both anticipate the reign of Messiah.

CONCLUSION

The Jewish calendar has tremendous significance for us. It recalls the great actions of God in our history and reminds us of all He has done for us. He is the Lord of history.

The holidays possess tremendous Messianic significance as well and highlight all that Yeshua has and will accomplish for us. They serve as excellent reminders for both Jews and Gentiles. But God has also used the holidays to preserve us as a people, a preservation in which we should actively participate by continuing to observe the Jewish calendar.

"In Jewish experience the holidays have yielded a double boon. They have been a bond of union, contributing mightily to the preservation of the Jewish people under circumstances that might have undone them.

"Being an extraterritorial group, Jewry always needed strong inner ties. The holy days have been such ties. . . .While the children of Israel preserved the Sabbath and the other sacred days, they found themselves preserved by them.

193

"But the sacred days did more than merely preserve Jewry; they breathed the sacred into Jewish life and endowed it with religious idealism ... 'I gave them ... to be a sign between Me and them, and that they might know that I am the Lord that sanctifieth them."

"... Thus have the holy days preserved Israel ... " (Beryl Cohon, *Judaism in Theory and Practice*, p. 170).

CHAPTER TWENTY-FOUR:

HOW TO PRAY
FOR THE PEACE
OF JERUSALEM . . .

Pray for the peace of Jerusalem: "May those who love you be secure" (Ps. 122:6).

1) There will only be peace in Jerusalem when all Israel is saved and the Jewish people say, "Blessed is he who comes in the name of the LORD." Pray for an outpouring of God's Spirit in Israel and for the Jewish people to repent of sin and to receive Jesus as LORD (Acts 1:8; Matt. 23:39; Rom. 11:26).

2) Pray for the Church worldwide to follow the Scriptural mandate to witness to the Jew first as we close in on the fullness of the Gentile age. Pray for peace in the Middle East, which can only occur when Jew and Arab recognize Jesus as LORD (Rom. 1:16; Luke 21:24; Is. 19:25).

3) Pray for quality Messianic Jews and all Jews to make Aliyah (return) to Israel and prepare the way for the return of the Messiah (Ezek. 37:12, 13).

4) Pray for housing, jobs, finances, health, safety, ease of immigration, no opposition from the religious, and supernatural ability to learn Hebrew for Messianic Jews in Israel (Deut. 28:1-3; Num. 14:9).

5) Pray for the lifting of the veil worldwide for Christians to be delivered from Replacement Theology (Rom. 11:17-21).

6) Pray for Jewish people to be protected from cult and occult groups. Pray for those already ensnared to be set free (Rom. 10:2).

7) Pray for abortion to be made illegal in Israel (Ps. 139: 13-16).

8) Pray for the establishment of many Messianic Jewish congregations and Bible schools in Israel. Pray for a spirit of unity among pastors (Eph. 4:3, 12).

9) Pray for Messianic Jews to be leaders in politics, business, the military and social reforms in Israel (Deut. 28:13; Esth. 10:3).

CHAPTER TWENTY-FIVE:

BLOW THE SHOFAR FOR ALIYAH

It's time for the Jew to make Aliyah (return) to Israel. Here are ten of over 700 Scriptures where God promises the Land of Canaan to His chosen people and commands or encourages them to return to the Land of Israel, which He gave to them as an everlasting inheritance.

Therefore this is what the Sovereign LORD says: I will now bring Jacob back from captivity and will have compassion on all the people of Israel, and I will be zealous for my holy name. They will forget their shame and all the unfaithfulness they showed toward me when they lived in safety in their land with no one to make them afraid. When I have brought them back from the nations and have gathered them from the countries of their enemies, I will show myself holy through them in the sight of many nations. Then they will know that I am the LORD their

God, for though I sent them into exile among the nations, I will gather them to their own land, not leaving any behind. I will no longer hide my face from them, for I will pour out my Spirit on the house of Israel, declares the Sovereign LORD (Ezek. 39: 25-29).

Come, O Zion! Escape, you who live in the Daughter of Babylon! (Zech. 2:7).

"I am with you and will save you," declares the LORD. "Though I completely destroy all the nations among which I scatter you, I will not completely destroy you. I will discipline you but only with justice; I will not let you go entirely unpunished" (Jer. 30:11).

Come out of her, my people! Run for your lives! Run from the fierce anger of the LORD.... You who have escaped the sword, leave and do not linger! Remember the LORD in a distant land and think on Jerusalem (Jer. 51:45, 50).

Those who cling to worthless idols [comforts of Babylon] forfeit the grace that could be theirs (Jon. 2:8).

Shake off your dust; rise up, sit enthroned, O Jerusalem. Free yourself from the chains on your neck, O captive Daughter of Zion. For this is what the LORD says: "You were sold for nothing, and without money you will be redeemed" (Is. 52:2,3).

Set up road signs; put up guideposts. Take note of the highway, the road that you may take. Return, O Virgin Israel, return to your towns (Jer. 31:21).

"However, the days are coming," declares the LORD, "when men will no longer say, 'As surely as the LORD lives, who brought the Israelites up out of the land of Egypt,' but they will say, 'As surely as the LORD lives, who brought the Israelites up out of the land of the north and out of all the countries where he had banished them.' For I will restore them to the land I gave their forefathers. But now I will send for many fishermen," declares the LORD, "and they will catch them. After that I will send for many hunters, and they will hunt them down on every mountain and hill and from the crevices of the rocks" (Jer. 16:14-16).

And everyone who calls on the name of the LORD will be saved; for on Mount Zion and in Jerusalem there will be deliverance, as the LORD has said, among the survivors whom the LORD calls (Joel 2:32).

The ransomed of the LORD will return. They will enter Zion with singing; everlasting joy will crown their heads. Gladness and joy will overtake them, and sorrow and sighing will flee away (Is. 51:11).

PART IV

IS THE CHURCH THE

"NEW ISRAEL"?

Is the Church the "New Israel"?

A Biblical Analysis of the Teachings of "Replacement Theology"

by Keith Parker

The idea that the Church is the new Israel is not a new one, but recently it has made a big comeback in theological circles. The doctrine is called "Replacement Theology." It has nothing to do with spare-part surgery, even if it sounds that way. It refers to the view that the Church has finally and forever replaced Israel in the purposes of God.

The Purpose of This Article:

Our purpose in these pages is to define what the Replacement Doctrine actually says, and to ask whether it is in fact true to the teaching of Scripture. We shall ask, and seek to answer, the questions: "Do the Jewish people as such still have any significance in the plan of God?" "Is it still the will of God that they possess the historic land of Canaan?" "Does the modern state of Israel have prophetic significance, or is it an historic accident?"

Extreme View of Some CHRISTIANS:

At the start, let it be said that some extreme views of Christian "Israel-fanatics" may have provoked a certain cynicism about Israel in some Christian quarters. Let me make clear that this article is not out to argue an extreme case, such as that the policies of the modern state of Israel can never be wrong; but it does set out to establish what the Scriptures actually teach on the subject of Israel.

A Short Definition of the Replacement Doctrine:

1. Israel has been replaced by the Christian Church in the purposes of God, or, more precisely, the Church is the historic continuation of Israel.

2. The Jewish people are now no different from any other group, such as the English or Spanish: all of these groups need and can receive salvation in Jesus the Messiah.

3. Apart from repentance, the new birth, and incorporation into the Church, the Jews have no future, no hope and no calling.

4. The same is true for every other nation and group.

5. In this age, since Pentecost, "Israel" properly so-called IS the Church.

How the Replacement Theologians Argue Their Case:

1. TO BE A SON OF ABRAHAM IS TO HAVE FAITH IN JESUS THE MESSIAH. Galatians 3:29 shows that sonship to Abraham is seen in spiritual, not national terms.

2. The promise of Canaan to Abraham was only a "starter." The real promised land is the whole world. (See Rom.4:13. It will be the Church, not Israel, that inherits the world.)

3. The nation of Israel was only the seed of the future Church which would arise, incorporating people of all nations (Mal.1:11).

4. Jesus taught that the Jews would lose their spiritual privileges and be replaced by another people (Matt. 21:43). The question of the apostles in Acts 1:6 "Lord, are you at this time going to restore the kingdom to Israel?" displays ignorance of God's purposes, and Jesus ignores it in his reply.

5. A true Jew is anyone born of the Spirit, whether he is racially Gentile or Jewish (Rom. 2:28-29).

6. Paul shows that the Church is really the same "olive tree" as was Israel. Therefore, to distinguish between Israel and the Church is, strictly speaking, false. Indeed, people of Jewish origin need to be grafted back into the Church (Rom. 11:17-23).

7. All the promises made to Israel in the Old Testament, unless they were historically fulfilled before the coming of Jesus the Messiah, are now the property of the Christian Church. These promises should not be interpreted literally, or carnally, but spiritually and symbolically, so that references to Israel, Jerusalem, Zion and the Temple, when they are prophetic, really refer to the

Church (2 Cor. 1:20). In the New Testament, all these things are understood spiritually (see Gal. 4:21-26; 6:16; Eph. 2:19-22; Heb. 12:22).

Confirmation of the Above Statements:

The present writer has shared this statement of the "Replacement" position with two personal friends who hold this position, and who are respected ministers and sincere Christian brothers. One confirms every word written as a fair statement of what he would believe about Israel. The other agreed with most, but said that he believed in a future national conversion for Israel, and realized that "the devil is opposing the Jews and the State of Israel, so there must be a future for them." My own observation is that there is a spectrum of belief about Israel and its replacement by the Church. Not everyone would go to the same extremes about it. Also, there are people of God whose views are changing. Some who are now in the "Replacement" camp will move out of it, given time. The one thing we must not do is to personally attack Christians who differ from us on any issue. We can freely disagree with them, and question their arguments, but we must avoid bitterness.

The Attractions of Replacement Theology:

(a) It is historically well-rooted in the Church (Early Fathers, Luther, Reformers).

(b) It has an intellectual appeal, because it does not require literal interpretation of the Bible.

206

(c) It has a simplicity appeal, involving, as it does, only one continuous body of the redeemed from the time of Adam to the end.

(d) It has a freshness appeal, because it usually goes along with a view of the "last things" which cuts right through the sometimes fanciful end-time teachings which have been current in the Church over the last 100 or so years.

(e) It appeals to that side of human character which has difficulty in acceding to the specific election of others.

Having stated (fairly, we trust) the case which the adherents of the Replacement Doctrine would put forward, let us now consider how other Christians, who believe that Israel is special to God, would approach the subject.

A General Statement:

(a) Israel, that is, the descendants of Abraham via Isaac and Jacob, had, have, and will have a very important place in the historic purposes of God.

(b) By no means is it true that every Israelite has been, is, or will be saved.

(c) But, unlike any other nation before or since, Israel was specially marked out and chosen by God for His purposes.

(d) It was through this nation that the Messiah, Jesus of Nazareth, came into the world, and the scene of both the first and second comings of the Messiah are on their territory, i.e., within the boundaries of the land of Canaan.

(e) Individually, Jews, as well as Gentiles, can only be saved in this age through faith in the person of the Messiah, Jesus.

(f) Yet, even in their unsaved state, the Jews are a people especially favored by God.

(g) Historically, a large part of the nation, though by no means all, rejected Jesus as the Messiah, and for that reason they lost their land, and forfeited their destiny as priestly people *for a season.*

(h) Yet for all that time there has *always* been a number of Jews who came to know and love Jesus, though at the expense of being swallowed up in a Gentilised Church, and "losing" their Jewishness.

(i) The Jewish people are unique in human history: they retained their identity as a people, *despite* having no homeland or political structure, *despite* attempts at forcible conversion and genocide, and *despite* their own desires to be assimilated and to become indistinguishable from their Gentile neighbors. Amazingly, they are *still* a distinct people, both in their own eyes, and in those of the world. In Germany they became almost totally assimilated as Germans, yet there they faced the most savage genocide in their history. In Soviet Russia, where distinctions of religion are supposed to be meaningless, many of them are again feeling their identity as Jews.

(j) God made some very clear promises to the Jews as a people. How could He possibly redefine them to apply to another people without being charged with deviousness?

(k) Today more Jews are believing in Jesus as the Messiah than has been the case since the first century.

(l) The State of Israel is re-established, although yet in unbelief. It has been preserved remarkably, if not miraculously, through many crises, bearing the marks of God's providence.

(m) There is yet to be a time when Jews in large numbers will turn to Jesus in a national way, and these will be specially used in the evangelization of the world. In our day there are congregations of Hebrew-speaking Jews in Israeli cities proclaiming Jesus as Messiah and Savior to their own people. The biblical Festivals (Lev. 23) are also increasingly used as relevant occasions to witness to their faith in Jesus as the Messiah.

WHAT THE SCRIPTURES SAY ABOUT ISRAEL

1. The general pattern of Scripture is that its histories and its predictions are literal, even if occasionally trimmed with poetic and pictorial language. This can be checked by referring to hundreds of fulfilled predictions. Here are a few examples:

(a) The prophecy about the altar at Bethel, 1 Kings 13:2 gives the prediction, and 2 Kings 23:15-17 shows the fulfillment.

(b) Messiah will be born of a virgin (Is. 7:14).

(c) Messiah will be born in Bethlehem (Mic. 5:2). For those who spiritualize the prophecies it would not have mattered if he had been born in Birmingham!

(d) Messiah will ride into Jerusalem on a donkey (Zech. 9:9).

(e) Messiah will suffer excruciating pain at the hands of men (Ps. 22).

(f) Messiah will be killed and buried in a rich man's grave (Is. 53:8-9).

(g) Messiah will be alive again after his death (Is. 53:10).

2. If in the case of fulfilled prophecy the fulfillment is literal, then it is logical to expect the other predictions to be literal too. Thus, where God speaks of Jerusalem, Judah and Israel in the last days, we can safely accept that at face value. Jesus, for example, predicted the destruction of the TEMPLE, (Matt. 24:2), and that JERUSALEM would be dominated by the Gentiles until much later in history (Luke 21:24). HOW CAN THIS BE INTERPRETED OF THE CHURCH? In fact the predictions were respectively fulfilled in A.D. 70 and A.D. 1967. The Bible, of course, also refers to the "heavenly Jerusalem"; but there is no problem in understanding when it is speaking of literal Jerusalem, and when of the heavenly Jerusalem.

3. Meaning of "Israel" and "Jew" in the New Testament:

There are about 77 references to "Israel" in the New Testament. Taken in context, *all but one* clearly refer to the Jewish people, either historically, or in their unbelief, or as the believing remnant. The one reference which is controverted or opposed is Galatians 6:16, where Paul says, "Peace and mercy to all who follow this rule, and to the *Israel of God*." In view of the clear fact that the word "Israel" never refers to the Christian Church, it is far better to interpret Galatians 6:16 as referring to the body of Jews who believe in Jesus. Remember that a believing Jew is a member of two covenant peoples — the Church *and* Israel.

The word "Jew" or "Jews" occurs about 191 times. It always refers to the Jewish people, whether to those who rejected Messiah or those who accepted Him. It is *never* used to describe a Gentile Christian. Romans 2:28-29, far from *extending* the description of "Jews" to Gentile Christians, actually is *restricting* "true Jewishness" to those Jews who are circumcised of heart, i.e., who know Jesus and are born of the Spirit.

Paul kept a distinction between Jews and Gentiles in the Church. This is illustrated by his attitude to his two close colleagues Timothy and Titus; Timothy, who was a Jew, he *circumcised* (Acts 16:3), but Titus was *not* circumcised, because he was a Gentile (Gal. 2:3).

4. The Letters of James and Peter:

James addresses his letter to: "The twelve tribes in the Diaspora" (literal translation). Clearly he saw Jewish believers in Jesus as still Israelites. He refers to their meeting as a "synagogue" (2:2 literal Greek). It is understood by all scholars that James was writing to Jewish Believers. The apostle Peter, who was an apostle to the "circumcision," addresses his letters to "chosen exiles of the Diaspora" (1 Pet. 1:1 literal Greek). Writing to Jewish believers, he obviously felt that they retained their Jewishness and national identity.

5. The Teaching of the Apostle Paul:

Paul was a Jew, and also the chosen apostle to the Gentiles. His letter to the Romans is the theological heart of the New Testament. Chapters 9-11 contain his mature teaching about Israel. Look now in detail at what he says, and see that Paul *does not replace Israel by the Church.*

211

(a) The Jews, even in their rejection of Jesus, ARE Israelites (Rom. 9:4).

(b) To Israel still belong the *sonship*, the glory, the *covenants*, the giving of the law, the worship and the *promises* (Rom. 9:4).

(c) The main body of Israel has lost salvation through rejecting the Messiah (Rom. 9:30-33; 10:21).

(d) Paul desires and prays for their salvation (Rom. 10:1-4). There is absolutely no anti-Jewishness in Paul's heart — completely the opposite (Rom. 9:1-3).

(e) Israel is NOT finally rejected (Rom. 11:1-2).

(f) Even in Old Testament times, Israel always had *a chosen remnant* of true believers among a nation largely composed of unbelievers. In Paul's day it was just the same (Rom. 11:2-6).

(g) God has judicially blinded the unbelieving majority to the truth (Rom. 11:7-10).

(h) The majority of unbelieving Israel has been temporarily set aside to give an opportunity of salvation to the Gentiles. But Gentile salvation is itself meant to provoke Israel to envy (Rom. 11:11).

(i) Israel has paid the price of rejection to give the Gentiles a chance. However, their restoration is assured, and will be "*life from the dead*" (Rom. 11:12-16).

(j) Unbelieving Jews are like olive branches cut off from their own tree. Believing Gentiles are wild olive branches grafted in. But Gentiles are not to boast against Jews. The *olive root* must mean the spiritual riches which flow from God via the patriarchs, which the Church now enjoys, and which unbelieving Israel has temporarily lost (Rom. 11:17-24).

(k) A future national repentance is expected for Israel. This is laid before us as "*a mystery*" (a secret which can now be revealed). It would be no amazing mystery if Paul were merely saying that all the elect will be saved! We already know that (Rom. 11:25-27). (Compare Zech. 12:10, where the prophet also speaks of a national repentance of Israel towards the Messiah.)

(l) Israel, *even in its unbelief,* is chosen, and loved by God (Rom. 11:28).

(m) They are "*enemies on your account*" — i.e., as a nation, they have been a kind of scapegoat, just as their Messiah, Jesus, was. Of course, Jesus was a sinless scapegoat, and that can by no means be claimed for Israel (Rom. 11:28). This alone should bring about great thankfulness towards the Jews from the Gentile Christians.

(n) "*God's gifts and his call are irrevocable.*" This is one of the firm grounds on which to believe that God has not replaced Israel by the Church (Rom. 11:29).

(o) Paul continues to identify himself as a Jew after receiving the fullness of redemption in Jesus, Israel's Messiah (Acts 21:39).

(p) The New Testament letter addressed to the "Hebrews" clearly underlines their continued identity as Jews even after coming to faith!

6. The Teaching of Jesus:

Our Lord Jesus does not teach the permanent rejection of Israel. He told the parable of the Tenants of the Vineyard in Matthew

21:33-44. In it he said, "*The kingdom of God will be taken away from you and given to people who will produce its fruit.*" But this is not a threat to the Jewish people as such — rather it is against their rulers, the chief priests and the Pharisees (see v. 45). In fact, Jesus foresees a time when the Jewish inhabitants of Jerusalem *will* accept his Messiahship, and this will herald his return (Matt. 23:37-39). Jesus promises the apostles that they will rule the twelve tribes of Israel (Matt. 19:28; Luke 22:30). Our Lord's first mission was to Israel rather than to the Gentiles (Matt. 10:5-6).

7. The Promises of God to the Jews:

God made a solemn promise of the land of Canaan to Abraham (Gen. 15:18-21). This promise is re-iterated in seven-fold affirmation in Psalm 105:8-10. Reading this passage carefully, it is hard to spiritually apply it to the Church! Indeed, if such violence can be done to clear statements of God, then the apparent promises made to the Church in the New Testament would likewise be capable of reinterpretation, and of re-application to some new people. (Why not the Muslims, who claim to have replaced the Church?)

Looking closer at Psalm 105: "He remembers his covenant forever, the word he commanded, for a thousand generations" (v. 8). This speaks in strongest terms of the perpetuity of God's promises. If one generation lasted only 40 years, that would make the territorial promise to Israel a 40,000-year lease!

"*The covenant he made with Abraham, the oath he swore to Isaac. He confirmed it to Jacob as a decree, to Israel as an everlasting covenant: 'To you I will give the land of Canaan as the portion you will inherit.'*" (v. 9-11). These words, "*covenant,*" "*oath,*" "*decree,*"

214

"everlasting covenant," if they have any meaning, must surely show the clear will of God that Israel should possess the land of Canaan.

8. God's Plan for Israel:

(a) God's purpose for Israel has always depended upon His initiative and election and upon Israel's response as a righteous nation (Deut. 7). Israel is promised abundant blessing when living in a righteous relationship with God (Lev. 26:1-13; Deut. 28:1-14), but God promised discipline (not rejection) when the nation rebelled (Lev. 26:14-46; Deut. 28:15-68). Scattering among the nations was the ultimate disciplinary measure with the promise of regathering to ultimately fulfill His purpose (Deut. 30).

God promised David a royal dynasty reaching eternal dimensions in Israel's Messiah (2 Sam. 7:11-17; 1 Chr. 17:10-15). Matthew demonstrates that Jesus of Nazareth is that Messiah (Matt. 1:1-16), and to John it is revealed that after Jesus' death and resurrection He is still the Davidic King of the Jews (Rev. 5:5; 22:16).

When God promised the New Covenant to the Jewish people (Jer. 31:31), He not only described the nature of this covenant, but promised there would be a day when the Jewish people "will all know me, from the least of them to the greatest" and will be righteous (Jer. 31:33-34). Since such a revival has never occurred in Israel's history, this event is yet to happen.

Through Ezekiel, God precisely confirms His purposes with Israel. Referring to Israel's restoration in chapter 36 alone, God is described 14 times as the "Sovereign LORD" who declares 22 times "I will" do it. Israel's God states what He will do:

(i) He will judge the nations for ill-treating Israel (36:3-7).

(ii) He will regather Israel to their promised land, which will prosper and be rebuilt and they will dwell in security (36:8-15).

(iii) He will judge Israel for "shedding blood" in the land, for preferring idols and for "profaning" God's name among the nations (36:16-21).

(iv) He will make Israel righteous for the sake of His holy name, not for Israel's sake (36:22).

(v) As a result of Israel's righteousness, God will demonstrate to the nations that He is the LORD (36:23-28).

(vi) When all this has occurred, Israel will know rich spiritual and material blessing (36:29-38), a promise which Paul succinctly describes as "life from the dead" (Rom. 11:15).

(b) God has NO plan to replace Israel.

Let us consider the following sample promises, and pose the question, "How ever could these words be transferred to the Christian Church?"

"Only if the heavens above can be measured and the foundations of the earth below be searched out will I reject all the descendants of Israel because of all they have done." (Jer. 31:37).

"I will surely gather them from all the lands where I banish them ... I will bring them back to this place... They will be my people, and I will be their God. I will give them singleness of heart and action, so that they will always fear me for their own good ...

216

I will make an everlasting covenant with them: I will never stop doing good to them, and I will inspire them to fear me, so that they will never turn away from me. I will . . . assuredly plant them in this land with all my heart and soul" (Jer. 32:37-41).

"Have you not noticed that these people are saying, 'The LORD has rejected the two kingdoms [i.e., Judah and Israel] he chose'? So they despise my people and no longer regard them as a nation. This is what the Lord says: 'If I have not established my covenant with day and night and the fixed laws of heaven and earth, then I will reject the descendants of Jacob and David my servant and will not choose one of his sons to rule over the descendants of Abraham, Isaac and Jacob. For I will restore their fortunes and have compassion on them'" (Jer. 33:24-26).

Surely if words bear any meaning at all, and if God does not speak in indecipherable riddles, these promises must guarantee a spiritual and territorial future to the Jews, and in no way make room for their replacement by any other people.

9. The Promises of God to His Church:

Let us consider only two of the many promises made to the Church:

". . . and on this rock I will build my church, and the gates of Hades will not overcome it" (Matt. 16:18).

In him we were also chosen, having been predestined according to the plan of him who works out everything in conformity with the purpose of his will, in order that we, who were the first to

217

hope in Messiah, might be for the praise of his glory. And you also were included in Messiah when you heard the word of truth, the gospel of your salvation. Having believed, you were marked in him with a seal, the promised Holy Spirit, who is a deposit guaranteeing our inheritance until the redemption of those who are God's possession — to the praise of his glory (Eph. 1:11-14).

If the clearly worded promises to Israel can be transferred, then how can we Christians have any confidence that the promises given to us, His Church, will not be somehow given to another people? We need to recognize that God's faithfulness to His promises to the Church is dependent upon His faithfulness to His promises to Israel. The Church is "grafted in" to the Olive tree, the Israel of God (Rom. 11:7-24) and the Church's members are citizens of the commonwealth of Israel (Eph. 2:11-19). How then can we doubt the equally specific promises of grace and election to Israel? If we do, we are being inconsistent in our reading of Scripture and undermining the very foundation of the Church.

Church History and Israel

Among the early Church Fathers, there were those who saw a future for Israel. Irenaeus was one. Many others were rabidly anti-Jewish, as was Martin Luther, the Reformer, in his later years. However, many godly Christian leaders believed what has been argued in these pages — men such as the theologian Bengel, the Wesley brothers, Horatio Bonar, Isaac Watts and Charles Spurgeon, to name only a few.

CONCLUSION

The whole dealing of God with Israel has been mysterious. Indeed, His purpose with the Church was mysterious also. It was unknown before the first century A.D., as Paul says in Ephesians 3:2-6.

If Israel's leaders had not rejected Jesus, if Jesus had not died, there would have been no atonement, and, hypothetically, no salvation, either for Jew or Gentile. Both the blindness of Israel and the corruption of Pilate were necessary to bring about God's redemption of the human race.

In light of all that has been set forth in these pages, should we be amazed that God has decreed the re-establishment of the territorial state of Israel or that there are now so many congregations of "Messianic Jews," or Jews believing in Jesus? Both the state of Israel and the calling out of Jewish assemblies are a clear sign to believers that God's purposes are working out, and that exciting though difficult times are in view for both the Church and Israel. Surely we should begin to lift up our heads for the Redemption that draws near!

Suggested further reading:

The Rebirth and Restoration of Israel (Rev. Murray Dixon);
Why Pray for Israel? (Ken Burnett)

PRAYER FOR ISRAEL P.O. Box No. 1 Golant, Cornwall United Kingdom

To receive a complimentary six-month subscription to the Messianic Vision newsletter, write to:

Messianic Vision
P.O. Box 34444
Bethesda, MD 20827